Oslo Manual on Select Topics of the Law of Armed Conflict

Yoram Dinstein • Arne Willy Dahl

Oslo Manual on Select Topics of the Law of Armed Conflict

Rules and Commentary

Springer Open

Yoram Dinstein
Tel Aviv University
Tel Aviv, Israel

Arne Willy Dahl
Nittedal, Norway

ISBN 978-3-030-39168-3 ISBN 978-3-030-39169-0 (eBook)
https://doi.org/10.1007/978-3-030-39169-0

This book is an open access publication.

This Springer imprint is published by the registered company Springer Nature Switzerland AG.
The registered company address is: Gewerbestrasse 11, 6330 Cham, Switzerland

Introduction

The Background of the Project

The *HPCR Manual on International Law Applicable to Air and Missile Warfare* (hereinafter the *HPCR Manual)* was adopted in 2009 by a Group of Experts and launched the following year with a Commentary.[1] The manual served as the basis for a series of courses—the AMPLE program—which for three years was funded by the Swiss Government and for one additional year by the Norwegian Government.[2] Instructors were largely drawn from the drafting committee of the *HPCR Manual*.

After sixteen courses, the AMPLE team of instructors summarized their experiences and concluded that the *HPCR Manual* was in need of updating for three main reasons. The first was that certain topics had been left out altogether, such as space warfare and autonomous weapons. The second was that, in some sections (for instance, protection of the natural environment), the consensus compromise reached by the Group of Experts was deemed unsatisfactory. The third was that events after the adoption of the manual showed that certain issues (e.g., protection of civilian airliners in conflict areas) deserved closer attention.

The AMPLE team of instructors approached the Norwegian Ministry of Defence (MoD) with a proposal for a research grant leading to a new manual on a list of selected topics. The Norwegian MoD was prepared to support the project on a limited basis. This meant that it would not be possible to gather all the experts involved in the *HPCR Manual* process. Instead of working on an update of that manual, it was decided to prepare a separate and independent document. It was also decided to go beyond air and missile warfare (including outer space), notably by including some sections on underwater operations. In still other sections, the focus was shifted from air and missile warfare to a more general approach.

[1]HPCR stands for the Program on Humanitarian Policy and Conflict Research at Harvard University.

[2]AMPLE stands for Air and Missile warfare Program of Legal Education.

The work on the new project took place exclusively in Oslo, and it was decided to name the final product the *Oslo Manual on Select Problems of the Law of Armed Conflict* (hereinafter the *Oslo Manual*). The *Oslo Manual* uses both the *HPCR Manual* and the *1994 San Remo Manual on International Law Applicable to Armed Conflicts at Sea* as models. Like them, the *Oslo Manual* must not be confused with a draft treaty intended to be used by a future diplomatic conference. The goal is rather to present a methodical restatement of existing international law on the selected topics, based on the general practice of States and treaties in force. No attempt has been made to be innovative or to come up with a *lex ferenda* (however desirable this may appear to be): the sole aim has been to systematically capture in the text the *lex lata* as we see it.

The views expressed in the *Oslo Manual* are the sole responsibility of the Group of Experts involved in the project and, notwithstanding the funding from the Norwegian Ministry of Defence, do not necessarily reflect the views of the Government of Norway.

The Process

The Norwegian MoD appointed Professor (Emeritus) Yoram Dinstein as academic director and Judge Advocate General (ret.) Arne Willy Dahl as project manager. The Norwegian Defence University College agreed to provide administrative services and has also given invaluable support in the drafting process.

A group of 15 experts were convened, based on professional ability, all of them participating in the project in their purely personal capacity (the names of all the experts appear in Appendix I). The Norwegian MoD followed the project via an observer, and there were also a few other observers present, in particular from the Norwegian Defence University College. The views expressed in the *Oslo Manual* do not necessarily reflect those of the governments or institutions for which some of the experts participating in the project are working.

The first meeting of the Group of Experts took place at the Norwegian Defence University College in December 2015. At this meeting a list of 12 topics was adopted and assigned to individual experts, with a view to the preparation of research papers (roughly matching sections of the emerging *Oslo Manual*). Later, some of the topics were split into two or more parts and a few additional topics added, bringing the total number of sections to 18.

Subsequent meetings of the Group of Experts took place in June and November 2016, with a final meeting in June 2017. After the November 2016 meeting, a drafting committee (the names of the members of which appear in Appendix II) was convened. It met several times during the winter, offering textual additions and emendations, as well as examining draft commentaries originally provided by the respective experts. The entire Group of Experts was given an opportunity to offer feedback throughout the work in progress of the drafting committee.

At the final meeting of the Group of Experts in June 2017, the Black-letter Rules were adopted by consensus and the draft Commentary discussed. The Commentary was updated by the drafting committee thereafter.

In the preparation of the *HPCR Manual* and the 1994 *San Remo Manual*, governments were represented. This was not the case with regard to the Group of Experts preparing the *Oslo Manual*. For this reason, it was found necessary to consult certain governments. This was done at meetings in Washington D.C. in October and in The Hague in December 2017. The ICRC was also approached with a view to hear their views. As a result of the oral consultations, some changes were made immediately and the amended text circulated to the Group of Experts.

The governments that had been consulted were offered to submit written comments, which were considered by the drafting committee together with comments by some members of the Group of Experts at meetings in April and June 2018. The comments necessitated some revision of the text, but with regard to the substance, changes in the *Oslo Manual* were generally limited to adjust to the fact that there are different views among States on certain questions and that it is for such reasons more difficult to draw conclusions about customary law in these matters. A chapeau was added to several strongly affected sections in order to explain the situation.

The Purpose of the Oslo Manual and its Commentary

It is hoped that the *Oslo Manual*, although it does not have a binding force, will serve as a valuable new restatement of the law of armed conflict. As such, it may prove useful in the development of future rules of engagement, the formulation of domestic military manuals, the preparation of training courses, and – above all – the actual conduct of armed forces in combat operations. The objective of the *Oslo Manual* is to be of help to those who plan, approve, or execute military operations before rather than after the event.

The Black-Letter Rules of the Oslo Manual

The Black-Letter Rules of the *Oslo Manual* are a collaborative effort of the Group of Experts involved in the project. There are 18 sections of varying lengths, depending on the "density" of State practice and the consequent number of norms that have been consolidated in each sphere. Consideration of the needs of users has also led to the elaboration in greater detail of some sections. The first six sections are high-tech (and in part even futuristic) in their orientation. They are interconnected in the sense that cybernetics is an important ingredient in outer space operations or in the use of remotely controlled weapons, and it is an integral part of autonomous weapons. In undersea systems, autonomy is more developed than in airborne and surface systems, due to the difficulties in passing signals for remote control through water.

The subsequent sections are less reliant on high-tech, but the emphasis throughout is on relatively recent developments in military operations. Occasionally, there are high-tech dimensions even here (by way of illustration, the increasing tendency to use civilian employees of the government, or civilian contractors, to fulfill remote-control combat functions).

The *Oslo Manual* includes a section on international criminal law. The principal reason is the need expressed by operators and legal advisers at the AMPLE courses for guidance with regard to their particular roles and responsibilities in a complex military environment. Familiarity with what the law of armed conflict requires no longer seems to suffice: military personnel wish to know the extent of individual accountability in planning and executing operations, gathering intelligence, evaluating expected collateral damage compared to anticipated military advantage, and so forth.

The Accompanying Commentary

Each Black-Letter Rule of the *Oslo Manual* is accompanied by a Commentary. This is aimed at providing user-friendly brief explanations for both legal advisers and military officers who plan, approve, or execute operations. Legal cites are kept to a minimum and the Commentary avoids academic discourses.

Although the Commentary was formulated by a small drafting committee (see above), this work was carried out in close cooperation with all the members of the Group of Experts. All participants had an opportunity to see the Commentary as it evolved and to critique it. Still, for obvious practical purposes, it was impossible to seek a line-by-line approval of a rather lengthy text by the entire Group of Experts. Hence, whereas the Black-letter Rules of the *Oslo Manual* reflect the views of the Group of Experts as a whole, the Commentary must be seen as the sole responsibility of the drafting committee.

Contents

Section I: Outer Space

Rule 1
For the purposes of this Manual:

(a) "Outer Space"

i. begins at the lowest possible point of the orbital perigee of artificial satellites;
ii. lies beyond the jurisdiction of all States.

Commentary

1. There is no general international agreement or customary international law specifying the precise definition and delimitation of Outer Space. The definition of "Outer Space" used in this Manual is consistent with current practice.
2. Outer Space with respect to jurisdictional arrangements is similar to the high seas.
3. At present, the lowest orbital perigee of satellites is approximately 100 km above sea level.[1]

(b) The Moon and other Celestial Bodies

i. do not include Earth.
ii. are separated by Outer Space but are not *stricto sensu* part of it.

Commentary

1. The Moon and other Celestial Bodies are generally considered *res communis omnium.* This implies that they are open for exploration, exploitation and use by

[1]As to the 100 kilometre approximation, see Program on Humanitarian Policy and Conflict Research at Harvard University, *HPCR Manual on International Law Applicable to Air and Missile Warfare* (AMW Manual) (2009), commentary Rule 1 (a) paragraph 5.

Y. Dinstein, A. W. Dahl, *Oslo Manual on Select Topics of the Law of Armed Conflict*,
https://doi.org/10.1007/978-3-030-39169-0_1

States, whether individually or collectively. They are not subject to national appropriation, which means that sovereignty can not be excercised over them by way of occupation (the non-appropriation principle).[2]
2. The non-appropriation principle implies a freedom of movement where States can launch objects, including spacecraft into Outer Space in order to orbit Earth, the Moon or other Celestial Bodies without having to seek permission from other States as long as the launch trajectory does not transit the national airspace of another State without authorization.
3. On the responsibility of States for activities conducted by persons belonging to their armed forces, see Rule 5.
4. The primary interest recognized in the OST is the maintenance of international peace and security.[3] See also Commentary to Rule 2.

(c) "Outer Space operations" are operations that employ capabilities aimed at achieving objectives in or through Outer Space.

Commentary
1. The phrase "Outer Space operations" is broadly defined in this Manual.[4]
2. Outer Space operations comprise activities where, for example, an object traverses temporarily through Outer Space as part of a ballistic trajectory, or where activities on Earth have effects in Outer Space, such as the launching of a satellite. Use of satellite signals on Earth, including for communication or navigation (including GPS and communication signals), is not an Outer Space operation. The jamming of a satellite is an Outer Space operation, whereas conventional jamming within airspace of a signal transmitted by a satellite is not.
3. Satellites send information via the electromagnetic spectrum, which is the collective term for all known frequencies of electromagnetic radiation and their linked photon wavelengths. The use of satellites can include the following categories: remote sensing, communications, scientific research and navigation. Most terrestrial use of satellite imagery, communication or navigation, however, does not constitute Outer Space operations as such.

(d) "Outer Space systems and assests" are those human-made systems and assets located in Outer Space as well as on the Moon and other Celestial Bodies, with or without human occupants. The phrase includes spacecraft, satellites and all related infrastructure (including up-links and down-links).

---

[2]Treaty on Principles Governing the Activities of States in the Exploration and Use of Outer Space, including the Moon and Other Celestial Bodies (OST) (1967), *United Nations Treaty Series (UNTS)*, vol. 610, page 205. See Articles I and II.

[3]OST, *ibid,* Article III.

[4]OST, *ibid,* Articles VI and VII.

Commentary

1. "Outer Space systems and assets" create the capabilities for Outer Space operations as defined in (c).
2. The definition of "Outer Space systems and assets" includes any or all component parts of the systems and assets as defined.
3. Examples are data and communication links, payloads, and ancillary devices and facilities such as:

   a. Ground stations;
   b. Ground station mission or user terminals, which may include initial reception, processing and exploitation terminals;
   c. Launch systems and directly related support infrastructure, including space surveillance, battle management, command, control, and communications infrastructure and computers;
   d. Launch sites;
   e. Booster storage facilities;
   f. Satellite storage and assembly facilities;
   g. Telemetry, Tracking, and Commanding (TT&C) nodes, including both hot and cold back up facilities;
   h. Research and development facilities; and
   i. Launch facilities and vehicles.

4. Manufacturing plants and assembly lines on Earth are generally excluded from the definition. However, exceptionally, all infrastructure essential for Outer Space operations, even if located on Earth, would be included.

Rule 2
Outer Space operations are governed by international law, including the Charter of the United Nations and the applicable principles and rules of the Law of Armed Conflict (LOAC).

Commentary

1. It has to be acknowledged that the degree of practice of States (as well as the state of *opinio juris*) leaves some doubt as to whether customary international law has already consolidated in so far Outer Space operations are concerned. However, in principle, all Outer Space operations are governed by the Charter of the United Nations.[5]
2. Article III of the Outer Space Treaty refers to the applicability in Outer Space of international law. The Group of Experts believes that the general reference to international law extends to LOAC. In view of the unique characteristics of Outer Space activities as such, in the absence of sufficient State practice and *opinio*

---

[5]Charter of the United Nations (1945), *UNTS,* vol. 1.

juris, the application or interpretation of LOAC in Outer Space may be subject to controversy.

3. The OST ostensibly limits the use of Outer Space to "peaceful purposes"[6] and the use of the Moon and other Celestial Bodies to "exclusively peaceful purposes".[7] This terminology is generally construed as proscribing only military operations that are carried out in breach of the Charter of the United Nations. The Charter explicitly recognizes the exercise of self-defence in response to armed attack (Article 51) and authorizes enforcement measures taken or authorized by the Security Council (under chapter "Section VII: Civilians Directly Participating in Hostilities").
4. The OST specifically prohibits the establishment of military bases, installations and fortifications as well as testing of any types of weapons and the conduct of military manoeuvres, on the Moon and other Celestial Bodies.
5. LOAC comprises both customary law and treaties. Customary law generally applies to all States. As far as treaties are concerned, they are binding only upon contracting parties. The reference to applicable principles and rules of LOAC is intended to emphasize that States are bound by different LOAC treaties and by applicable customary law. However, which principles and rules of LOAC apply, and how they apply, may depend, *inter alia*, on the classification of an act as an attack under LOAC.

Rule 3

State Parties to the Outer Space Treaty must not place in orbit around the Earth any objects carrying nuclear weapons or any other weapons of mass destruction, install such weapons on the Moon or other Celestial Bodies, or station such weapons in Outer Space in any other manner.

Commentary

1. This Rule is based on Article IV of the OST which relates to nuclear weapons and other weapons of mass destruction (WMD). The Group of Experts believes that Article IV of the OST today reflects an emerging customary international norm.
2. In order to be considered to be "placed in orbit" an Outer Space object must complete at least one orbit. WMD or nuclear weapons that simply transit through Outer Space without completing an orbit, such as an Intercontinental Ballistic Missile (ICBM), do not fall within the scope of the prohibition.
3. There is no generally accepted definition of WMD. Nuclear Weapons are not defined in international treaties, but according to an Advisory Opinion of the

[6] OST, see fn. 2, Preamble.
[7] OST, see fn. 2, Article IV(2).

International Court of Justice they are "explosive devices whose energy results from the fusion or fission of the atom".[8] The Group of Experts took the view that, for the purposes of Article IV (1) of the OST, WMD comprise—in addition to nuclear weapons—those weapons that are prohibited by the 1972 Biological Weapons Convention[9] and the 1993 Chemical Weapons Convention.[10]

4. An Outer Space object with a nuclear power source is not necessarily a nuclear weapon for the purposes of this Manual.

Rule 4

Without prejudice to the Charter of the United Nations, the principles and rules of LOAC are the *lex specialis* during armed conflict and prevail over the general law of Outer Space.

Commentary

1. The general legal regime applicable in Outer Space, based on customary law as well as applicable treaties, is peacetime law. The OST and other Outer Space treaties are silent as regards the possibility of an armed conflict.[11] However, LOAC is the *lex specialis* in the sense that it prevails in situations of armed conflict (either international or non-international) involving Outer Space operations over any inconsistent peacetime norm applicable in Outer Space. That said, LOAC cannot override the Charter of the United Nations.
2. By definition, the principles and rules of LOAC—which apply only in situations of armed conflict—are more specific than the peacetime principles and rules of the law of Outer Space which are *lex generalis*.

Rule 5

With respect to an armed conflict, States bear responsibility for their respective internationally wrongful Outer Space operations as well as other wrongful activities conducted in Outer Space that are attributable to them. Responsibility extends to such actions by all persons forming part of the armed forces.

Commentary

1. This Rule exclusively applies to State responsibility under LOAC. However, the first sentence of the Rule is also consistent with Article VI of the OST.

---

[8]Legality of the Threat or Use of Nuclear Weapons, Advisory Opinion, *I.C.J. Reports* 1996, p. 226, at para 35, page 243.

[9]Convention on the Prohibition of the Development, Production and Stockpiling of Bacteriological (Biological) and Toxin Weapons and on Their Destruction (BWC) (1972), *UNTS*, vol. 1015, page 164, Article I.

[10]Convention on the Prohibition of the Development, Production, Stockpiling and Use of Chemical Weapons and on their Destruction (CWC) (1993), *International Legal Materials* (*ILM*), vol. 32, page 800, Article II.

[11]See fn. 2.

2. This is also the general Rule of State responsibility as defined by the International Law Commission,[12] which are reflective of customary international law. The second sentence of the Rule is based on Article 3 of the 1907 Hague Convention (IV) and Article 91 of the 1977 Protocol I Additional to the Geneva Conventions (AP/I).[13]
3. It is the view of the Group of Experts that the 1972 Liability Convention does not apply between Belligerent States to an armed conflict.[14] The Liability Convention does however remain effective between a Belligerent State and Neutral States. See Rule 18.

Rule 6
A person who wrests control of Outer Space systems and assets assumes responsibility for subsequent use of the system in accordance with the degree and the duration of the control exercised.

Commentary
1. The Rule refers to the individual responsibility of the person who wrests control of Outer Space systems and assets. Should such a person act on behalf of a State, his/her act will be attributable to that State, which will bear State responsibility.
2. A person who wrests control of an Outer Space system and asset, will bear responsibility for the subsequent use for which the system and asset is put while that individual retains control. However, a question arises as to the allocation of responsibility when the person who wrests control of the system then tranfers that control to another person. There would be potential criminal liability if intent and knowledge could be established.
3. See Commentary to Rule 45.

Rule 7
(a) In the study, development, acquisition or adoption of a new weapon, means or method of Outer Space warfare, a State that is party to Additional Protocol I must determine whether its employment would,

---

[12]International Law Commission's Draft Articles on Responsibility of States for Internationally Wrongful Acts, Report of the International Law Commission on the work of its fifty-third session, *Yearbook of the International Law Commission,* 2001, Vol. II, Part Two, page 26, Articles 4 and 5.

[13]Convention IV Respecting the Laws and Customs of War on Land and its Annex: Regulations Respecting the Laws and Customs of War on Land (1907 Hague Regulations) (1907), Schindler and Toman, *The Laws of Armed Conflicts,* Martinus Nijhoff Publishers (Leiden/Boston) (2004), page 66. Protocol Additional to the Geneva Conventions of 12 August 1949, and Relating to the Protection of Victims of International Armed Conflicts (Protocol I), (AP/I) (1977), *The Laws of Armed Conflicts,* page 711.

[14]Convention on International Liability for Damage Caused by Space Objects, (Liability Convention) (1972), UNTS, vol. 961, page 187.

in some or all circumstances, be prohibited by any rule of international law applicable to that State.

(b) In the acquisition of a new weapon or means of Outer Space warfare, a State that is not party to Additional Protocol I should determine whether its employment would, in some or all circumstances, be prohibited by applicable principles and rules of LOAC.

Commentary

1. This Rule is based on Article 36 of AP/I, which is applicable only to Contracting Parties.
2. The provision of Article 36 of AP/I has not yet crystallized as customary international law, and therefore non-contracting Parties are not legally bound to abide by the full extent of its strictures. Some of the non-contracting Parties whose interests are specially affected, while conducting significant weapon review procedures, maintain that this is done as a "best practice" rather than out of a sense of legal obligation. In other words, these countries do not share an *opinio juris* on an independent obligation to conduct legal reviews of weapons under customary international law.
3. As far as non-contracting Parties to Additional Protocol I are concerned, the practice regarding the adoption of new methods of warfare is less clear than it is with regard to new means of warfare.
4. For its part, the Group of Experts believes that there is an implied rule requiring all States to review the lawfulness of new weapons and means of warfare that they acquire, with a view to avoiding incompatibility with the two basic principles of LOAC, *i.e.,* distinction and the prohibition of unnecessary suffering and superfluous injury.
5. The reference to the development or acquisition of a new means of warfare has to be understood as referring to the planned or intended consequence of that means of warfare in the context of its normal and expected use.
6. Reference to the principles and rules of LOAC does not obviate the need to conform with other norms of international law as and when applicable.
7. It may as well be added that the testing of nuclear weapons in Outer Space is specifically prohibited by the Treaty Banning Nuclear Weapon Tests in the Atmosphere, in Outer Space and Under Water.[15]

Rule 8

In Outer Space operations occurring during armed conflict, the concept of attack applies to all acts of violence against the adversary, whether in offence or defence. The acts must be intended to cause—or must be reasonably expected to result in—death, injury, destruction or damage. These acts

[15]Treaty Banning Nuclear Weapon Tests in the Atmosphere, in Outer Space and Under Water (LTBT) (1963), *UNTS,* vol. 480, page 44. Articles 1(a) and (b).

generally do not include those intended to cause only temporary loss of functionality, e.g., jamming.

Commentary

1. The first sentence, which is reflected in AP/I,[16] is based on customary law.
2. The notion of "attack" under this Rule must not be confused with *jus ad bellum* rules under the Charter of the United Nations.
3. The second sentence defines the term "acts of violence". Accordingly, the intentional destruction of an Outer Space object or the intentional infliction of any physical damage to it will be an attack under this Rule. Acts that are not intended to result in such consequences do not qualify as attacks.
4. "Acts of violence against the adversary" include acts against combatants or civilians, military objectives or civilian objects.
5. During military operations in armed conflict, many acts may be understood to have some causal connection to death, injury, destruction, or damage. Acts in support of military operations (e.g., refuelling military aircraft), accidents, or other acts that simply bear some causal connection to death, injury, destruction, or damage are not, by that causal connection, automatically considered attacks.
6. Nonetheless, where it is reasonably expected that the direct and ordinary consequence of an action is to cause death, injury, destruction or damage, such action could, depending on the circumstances, be regarded as "intentional" thus qualifying the action as an attack and thereby triggering the legal obligations that attach to "attacks" under LOAC.
7. Causing temporary loss of functionality, which could either be brief or prolonged—in and of itself—does not constitute an attack inasmuch as it usually does not cause death, injury, damage or destruction. However, in Outer Space, causing a temporary loss of functionality may in certain circumstances be intended to cause death, injury, destruction or damage, and would thus constitute an attack. For example, the temporary degradation of space assets', navigation functionality could be used intentionally to cause the crash of those assets. Conversely, temporary degradation resulting in only temporary consequences, such as temporary loss of communication, would not *per se* constitute an attack.
8. "Shadowing" of a satellite, which means depriving it of solar energy supply through positioning another object in between the satellite and the sun, does not necessarily constitute an attack. In the context of the present Rule and as regards what constitutes damage, there are divergent views. Some have said that damage must be limited specifically to a situation in which physical repairs are required, whereas others would contend that reduced or extinguished functionality would be sufficient.

---

[16] AP/I, see fn. 13, Article 49.

9. Similarly, "blinding" a satellite sensor by targeting it with a laser (and causing no physical damage to the satellite, but temporarily preventing its proper functioning), does not necessarily qualify as an attack.
10. Jamming, like the blinding of a sattelite, is a form of temporary loss of functionality. It should be noted, however, that jamming may be a constitutive component of an overall attack.

Rule 9

In principle, Outer Space systems and assets belonging to the armed forces constitute military objectives because, by nature, they make an effective contribution to the enemy's military action.

Commentary

1. Military objectives by nature are defined in chapter "Section IX: Military Objectives by Nature", Rules 77 ff.
2. Military objectives by nature are lawful targets at all times and in all circumstances during an armed conflict.
3. The words "in principle" were included to clarify that this was a general rule subject to exceptions. For example, medical aid stations in Outer Space belonging to the military would be excluded.
4. Outer Space systems and assets belonging to the armed forces may include, e.g.: military satellites performing telecommunication, Earth Observation (EO), early warning, weather observation, navigation, and Intelligence, Surveillance and Reconnaissance (ISR) functions. See commentary to Rule 1 (d).
5. Since infrastructure components may be located in a Neutral State, additional considerations apply, see Rules 18–19 and Commentary.

Rule 10

Civilian Outer Space systems and assets must not be the object of attack unless they qualify as military objectives—if not by nature—by location, purpose or use.

Commentary

1. Civilian objects are protected against direct attack according to customary LOAC. This is also the rule under Article 52(1) of AP/I. *Ex hypothesi,* civilian objects are not military objectives.
2. Civilian space systems include satellites and all related ground infrastructure that cannot be classified as a military objective according to Rule 9.
3. Civilian space systems will nevertheless become lawful targets if by location, purpose or use they make an effective contribution to military action, and if their total or partial destruction or neutralization, in the circumstances ruling at the time offers a definite military advantage.

4. Examples of purpose or use rendering civilian Outer Space systems and assets lawful targets are:
   a. Commercial space systems used to augment military space capabilities and to increase the resiliency of space architectures, e.g., space launch facilities.
   b. Communication satellites or commercial earth-imaging systems normally used for civilian purposes but effectively contributing to military action, e.g., GPS satellite systems and EO satellites used for military Command and Control functions or intelligence collection.
   c. Satellites hosting a military payload (dual use).

Rule 11
In Outer Space operations constituting attacks, assessments of collateral damage should take into consideration the effects of space debris expected to result from the attack.

Commentary

1. Rule 11 reflects unique Outer Space considerations regarding the proportionality rule as established by treaty and customary LOAC prohibiting attacks that may be "expected to cause incidental loss of civilian life, injury to civilians, damage to civilian objects, or a combination thereof, which would be excessive in relation to the concrete and direct military advantage anticipated."[17] "Collateral damage" is the common term for "incidental loss of civilian life, injury to civilians, damage to civilian objects, or a combination thereof", as expressed in Article 51(5)(b) of AP/I.
2. The fact that space debris can be expected to result from a kinetic attack in Outer Space does not in itself render the attack unlawful, but it may play a significant role in the assessment of collateral damage.[18]
3. Due to the particular nature of Outer Space, the debris expected to result from an attack or the effects of an electromagnetic pulse (EMP), could easily affect civilian satellites, or damage or destroy the Outer Space assets of the attacking Party itself.
4. The outcome of the proportionality assessment may depend upon the orbit where the attack occurs. For example, the effects of an attack by a Kinetic Anti-Satellite (K-ASAT) Weapon in the geostationary orbit could be particularly serious.
5. An attack upon an Outer Space system or asset may be expected to result in damage to or destruction of satellites not constituting military objectives.

---

[17] AP/I, see fn. 13, Article 51(5)(b).

[18] Space debris may be defined as all man-made objects, including fragments and elements thereof, in Earth orbit or re-entering the atmosphere, that are non-functional. See Space Debris Mitigation Guidelines of the Committee on the Peaceful Uses of Outer Space, endorsed by the UN Committee on the Peaceful Uses of Outer Space at its fiftieth session and contained in A/62/20, annex.

Moreover, an attack may result in the denial of the exercise of the right to use Outer Space by civilian satellites or seriously damage crucial civilian infrastructures that depend upon Outer Space systems in order to function properly. Such expected consequences must be considered in relation to the concrete and direct military advantage anticipated when applying the proportionality rule.

6. Collateral damage does not include mere inconvenience. However, if as a result of the presence of debris in Outer Space a civilian satellite is forced to detour, thereby expending fuel so as to be unable to perform its normal functions, the situation may no longer amount to mere inconvenience.

Rule 12
The concept of direct participation in hostilities applies to civilians, including civilian employees of State agencies, who conduct Outer Space operations in the context of an armed conflict.

Commentary

1. The concept of direct participation in hostilities (DPH) is firmly established in treaty and customary LOAC and is expressed in Article 51(3) of AP/I, as well as common Article 3 to the four Geneva Conventions and Article 13(3) of AP/II applicable in non-international armed conflicts.[19] In accordance with this concept, civilians enjoy protection from attack "unless and for such time as they take a direct part in hostilities."
2. This Rule is without prejudice to the question whether a certain activity actually qualifies as DPH.
3. See chapters "Section VII: Civilians Directly Participating in Hostilities" and "Section VIII: Civilians Participating in Unmanned Operations".

Rule 13
In Outer Space operations, activities qualifying as direct participation in hostilities may include:

(a) Any activity designed or intended to directly cause death of, injury to, damage to or destruction of to an adverse party;

[19]Protocol Additional to the Geneva Conventions of 12 August 1949, and Relating to the Protection of Victims of Non-International Armed Conflicts (Protocol II) (AP/II) (1977), *Laws of Armed Conflicts,* page 775, at page 781. Common Article 3 appears in the following: Convention (I) for the Amelioration of the Condition of the Wounded and Sick in Armed Forces in the Field (GC I) (1949), *Laws of Armed Conflict,* page 459, at page 461; Convention (II) for the Amelioration of the Condition of the Wounded, Sick and Shipwrecked Members of Armed Forces at Sea (GC II) (1949), *Laws of Armed Conflict,* page 485, at page 487; Convention (III) relative to the Treatment of Prisoners of War (GC III) (1949), *Laws of Armed Conflict,* page 507, at page 512; Convention (IV) Relative to the Protection of Civilian Persons in Time of War (GC IV), *Laws of Armed Conflict,* page 575, at page 580.

(b) Defence of military space objects against enemy attacks;
(c) Contributing to targeting procedures, such as helping to identify or prioritize targets;
(d) Engaging in planning specific attacks;
(e) Military reconnaissance or surveillance; or
(f) Operating a tactical communications relay.

Commentary

1. The entire issue of definition of activities amounting to DPH is subject to controversy and disagreement among experts. This Manual focuses on examples on which consensus could be reached.
2. This Rule too is without prejudice to the question whether a certain activity actually qualifies as DPH. On the notion of DPH, see chapter "Section VII: Civilians Directly Participating in Hostilities".

Rule 14

In Outer Space operations constituting attacks, feasible precautions should be taken with a view to the specific characteristics of Outer Space, including the presence or functions of civilian satellites and the effects on the use of the electromagnetic spectrum.

Commentary

1. The duty to take feasible precautions in attack is customary in nature and is reflected in Article 57 of AP/I. "Feasible precautions" are those that are practicable or practically possible, taking into account all circumstances ruling at the time, including humanitarian and military considerations. In particular, Belligerent States should verify that the target is a military objective and minimize collateral damage. When feasible, attacks must be cancelled or suspended if decision-makers learn that the object is not a military objective or if the attack may be expected to violate the proportionality rule.
2. When alternative targets of attack present themselves, the legal position as far as Contracting Parties to AP/I are concerned is that—among targets offering similar military advantage—they must select the one where collateral damage would be minimized. As far as non-contracting parties to AP/I are concerned, the obligation to minimize collateral damage in attack may be understood as applying only to targets offering the same military advantage.
3. Effective advance warning of attacks likely to affect the civilian population must be provided, unless circumstances do not permit.
4. Verification that a target is a military objective should take into account that civilian communications satellites often are placed in crowded orbits such as the geostationary orbit and that they may be controlled by a multitude of owners and third-party providers of services, in a variety of jurisdictions.

5. Commercial communication satellites usually have a capacity based on a multitude of transponders, where capacity, not transponders, is sold or leased to a multitude of clients. Military use of any such capacity renders that satellite a military objective. The fact that the use of the remaining capacity is civilian in nature does not affect the characterization of the satellite, but may raise proportionality issues.
6. The electromagnetic spectrum is defined in paragraph 3 of the Commentary to Rule 1(c) and is the medium for providing satellite-information and services to the Earth. Feasible precautions should be taken in order to reduce the extent of harmful effects on space capabilities that do not constitute military objectives.
7. The requirement to take precautions in attack necessitates assessment of the impact of space debris. It also might involve consideration of the effects on the use of the electromagnetic spectrum. The assessment includes efforts to assess the likelihood of civilian satellites being struck by debris (see Rule 11) and a consideration of limitations on the manoeuvre capabilities of Outer Space vehicles to the extent that this amounts to damage as distinct from mere inconvenience. It may also be appropriate to assess the effect of an energized atmosphere or scintillated ionosphere upon space communications and may require determination of the likelihood of interference or damage to be caused to a given signal, satellite, line of communication or ground asset by the effects on the electromagnetic environment.
8. If an Outer Space system or asset controlled by a Neutral State qualifies as a lawful target, additional considerations apply. See Rule 18 with Commentaries.

Rule 15
The AP/1 obligations with regard to the natural environment should apply to Outer Space operations and to their effects on all parts of Outer Space, the Moon and other Celestial Bodies.

Commentary

1. The provision of Article 35 (3) AP/1 protects the natural environment against attacks that are expected or intended to cause widespread, long-term and severe damage. This provision does not apply to Outer Space. However, the Group of Experts agreed that in the conduct of Outer Space operations the same principle should be applied by analogy.
2. For the meaning of the AP/1 prohibition, see the Commentary on Rule 140.
3. For an illustration relating to Outer Space, consider the irradiation of areas of Outer Space protected by the Van Allen belts through nuclear explosions.

Rule 16
States Parties to the ENMOD Convention are prohibited from making any military or other hostile use of Outer Space environmental modification

techniques having widespread, long-lasting or severe effects as the means of destruction, damage or injury to any other State Party.

Commentary

1. Because the ENMOD Convention[20] does not express customary LOAC, its obligations only bind States Parties to the Convention. The ENMOD Convention specifically prohibits the use of environmental modification techniques on the "lithosphere, hydrosphere and atmosphere, or of Outer Space."

Rule 17

(a) Enemy Outer Space systems and assets, in theory, could be subject to capture as prize.
(b) Enemy character can be determined by registration, ownership, charter, control, or other criteria.
(c) Neutral Outer Space systems and assets may not be captured as prize, unless they are used for rendering unneutral service.

Commentary

1. Subject to Rule 3, the LOAC right to capture of enemy Outer Space systems and assets prevails over the duty to recover and return space objects in the Rescue Agreement, Article 5.[21]
2. The use of "in theory" is intended to convey that the Group of Experts was not aware of State practice in subjecting space systems and assets to prize law. Moreover, capture of an object in orbit may be impractical under present technology.
3. The enemy character of an Outer Space system or asset is not necessarily the same as its "State of registry" according to the Registration treaty.[22]
4. In theory, rendering unneutral service would make neutral Outer Space systems and assets liable to be captured as prize. However, many of the services that are today provided by satellites (such as providing satellite imagery for military use) could, if provided to a Belligerent Party, render the satellite a lawful military objective rather than merely subjecting it to capture.

---

[20]Convention on the Prohibition of Military or any Hostile use of Environmental Modification Techniques (ENMOD) (1976), *UNTS*, vol. 1108, page 151.

[21]Agreement on the Rescue of Astronauts, the Return of Astronauts and Return of Objects Launched into Outer Space (1968), *UNTS*, vol. 672, page 119.

[22]Convention on Registration of Objects Launched into Outer Space (1974), *UNTS*, vol. 1023, page 15, Article 1(c).

Rule 18
As a general principle, neutral States must not knowingly allow space systems and assets for which they are responsible to be used by Belligerent States in Outer Space operations related to armed conflict.

Commentary

1. The concept of neutrality, applicable to a State which is not a Belligerent Party in a given international armed conflict, relates to the conduct of hostilities in all circumstances and therefore extends to Outer Space operations. This is particularly important as regards the obligation of the Neutral State to maintain its impartiality in the armed conflict.
2. Given that the law of neutrality relies heavily on the concept of "neutral territory", some aspects of that law may be inconsistent with the characteristic of Outer Space. The Group of Experts believe however, that the law of neutrality may be applied in the context of Outer Space *mutatis mutandis.*
3. There is substantive treaty law as well as customary law with respect to the standing of a Neutral State in an armed conflict. However, neither the treaty law nor customary law pertains to Outer Space as such. Hence, any application of existing rules in an Outer Space context can only be based on analogy.
4. This Rule reflects the principles of the customary law of neutrality (as expressed, *inter alia,* in the 1907 Hague Convention V on Neutral Powers and Persons in War on Land and the 1907 Hague Convention XIII on Neutrality in Naval War[23]).
5. Belligerent States are forbidden from erecting on the territory of a Neutral State any military ground infrastructure intended to be used in the armed conflict. This general prohibition also applies to communication installations for satellites operated by Belligerent armed forces.
6. The prohibition extends to the exclusively military use of such installations, established before the armed conflict on the territory of a Neutral State.[24]
7. The employment on neutral territory of ground station functions such as TT&C (see paragraph 5 of the Commentary to Rule 9) used for communication between a spacecraft and ground systems for the execution of belligerent acts is a violation of neutrality. However, the simple downloading of data from a civilian satellite by ground stations on neutral territory does not violate neutrality when the activity is not linked to the hostilities.
8. A Neutral State may not launch military satellites on behalf of a Belligerent Party. Nor may it provide any services to a Belligerent Party military satellite already in orbit.

---

[23]Convention (V) Respecting the Rights and Duties of Neutral Powers and Persons in Case of War on Land (1907), *Laws of Armed Conflicts,* page 1399. Convention (XIII) Concerning the Rights and Duties of Neutral Powers in Naval War (1907), *Laws of Armed Conflicts,* page 1407.

[24]For comparative purposes, see Article 3 of the 1907 Hague Convention (V) on Neutral Powers and Persons in War on Land, see fn. 23.

9. A Neutral State may not sell or otherwise transfer a satellite for military uses by a Belligerent Party.
10. However, commercial and trade activities by neutral companies or individuals with a Belligerent State are not prohibited.
11. The use by a Belligerent State of telecommunication satellites owned by or under the exclusive control of a Neutral State is not a violation of neutrality. A Neutral State has no obligation to prevent the use of its telecommunication satellites by a Belligerent State to the conflict which had access to the satellite prior to the outbreak of hostilities.[25]
12. Existing non-military telecommunications satellites owned by private companies or individuals may be used by Belligerent Parties, e.g., by renting satellite transponder capacity for voice and data communication of a military nature.
13. Restrictions imposed by a Neutral State on the belligerent use of privately owned telecommunication satellites, must be impartially applied to both (all) Belligerent Parties.[26]
14. The necessary use of force by a Neutral State to prevent its Outer Space assets from being used by a Belligerent State to commit a belligerent act is not a violation of neutrality.[27]
15. This Rule is without prejudice to Rules 9 and 10 and the definition of military objectives.

Rule 19
As a general principle, Belligerent States must conduct their Outer Space operations with due regard for the rights of Neutral States.

Commentary
1. There is an obligation incumbent on Belligerent States to act with due regard for the rights of Neutral States to use Outer Space.[28]
2. In the planning of Outer Space operations, Belligerent States should implement measures in order to reduce the risk of damaging neutral critical infrastructure and communication space assets.[29]

---

[25] 1907 Hague Convention (V) on Neutral Powers and Persons in War on Land, *ibid,* Article 8.

[26] 1907 Hague Convention (V) on Neutral Powers and Persons in War on Land, *ibid*, Article 9.

[27] 1907 Hague Convention (V) on Neutral Powers and Persons in War on Land, *ibid,* Article 10.

[28] OST, see fn. 2, Article IX.

[29] Similar duties are established in naval warfare. See San Remo Manual on International Law Applicable to Armed Conflicts at Sea (*San Remo Manual*) (1994), *The Laws of Armed Conflicts*, page 1153, paras 12 and 88.

Section II: Cyber Operations

At the time of composing the Oslo Manual, there were some fundamental differences of opinion among States as to the interpretation or acceptability of terms such as "cyber means of warfare", "cyber methods of warfare", and "cyber attacks". The Group of Experts took cognizance of those differences of opinion but concluded, coherent with the view of the International Court of Justice, as expressed in the *Nuclear Weapons* Advisory Opinion[1] that the cardinal principles of LOAC would apply to all forms of warfare. This includes cyber warfare.

Rule 20

(a) For the purposes of this Manual, "cyber operations" are operations that employ capabilities aimed at achieving objectives in or through cyberspace.

Commentary

1. The definition of cyber operations in this Rule is based on the definitions used in the US Joint Publications.[2] The reference to "primary purpose" in the US definition is omitted from the present Rule, as it is believed that it unnecessarily restricts the definition.
2. The fact that objectives are achieved "in or through" cyberspace means that the operations covered by the present definition include both those the effects of which are confined to cyberspace and those that have effects in the physical world through the manipulation, deletion or corruption of data.
3. The kinetic bombardment of physical cyber infrastructures would not be a cyber operation for the purposes of the present Rules.

[1]See chapter "Section I: Outer Space", fn. 8.

[2]US Chairman of the Joint Chiefs of Staff, Joint Publication 3-0, Joint Operations, 17 January 2017, page GL-8. See also U.S Chairman of the Joint Chiefs of Staff, Joint Publication 3-12 (R), Cyberspace Operations, 5 February 2013.

Y. Dinstein, A. W. Dahl, *Oslo Manual on Select Topics of the Law of Armed Conflict*,
https://doi.org/10.1007/978-3-030-39169-0_2

4. "Cyber operations" as defined in this Rule include:
    a. Unauthorized access to computers, computer systems or networks to obtain information, but without necessarily affecting the functionality of the accessed system or amending, corrupting, or deleting the data resident therein; *and*
    b. Operations, whether in offence or in defence, intended to alter, delete, corrupt or deny access to computer data or software for the purposes of propaganda or deception; partly or totally disrupting the functioning of the targeted computer, computer system or network and related computer-operated physical infrastructure (if any); or producing physical damage extrinsic to the computer, computer system, or network.
5. "Cyberspace" is understood in this Rule as "a global domain within the information environment consisting of the interdependent network of information technology infrastructures and resident data, including the Internet, telecommunications networks, computer systems, and embedded processors and controllers."[3]

(b) Cyber operations, when carried out as part of an armed conflict, are governed by applicable principles and rules of LOAC.

Commentary

1. This Rule is limited to armed conflict, whether international or non-international.
2. Paragraph 5 of the Commentary to Rule 2 explains the import of the phrase "applicable principles and rules of LOAC".
3. The expression "when carried out as part of an armed conflict" was included in order to exclude cyber operations falling outside the scope of the armed conflict.[4]

Rule 21
With respect to an armed conflict, States bear responsibility for their cyber operations as well as other activities conducted in cyberspace that are attributable to them. Such responsibility includes actions by all persons belonging to the armed forces of the State.

---

[3]US Department of Defence, Dictionary of Military and Associated Terms, Joint Publication 1-02, 8 November 2010 (as amended through 15 February 2016), page 58.

[4]The applicability of LOAC to cyber operations has been affirmed, *inter alia*, in the Report of Governmental Experts on Developments in the Field of Information and Telecommunications in the Context of International Security, 22 July 2015, UN Doc. A/70/174, page 13 and the Department of Defence Law of War Manual *(US DoD Manual)* (2015, amended 2016), at page 1013 ff.

Commentary

1. This Rule deals with State responsibility, which applies in the relations between an injured State and a wrong-doing State. Hence, its applicability would generally be confined to international armed conflicts. However, in some situations, State responsibility vis-a-vis other States will also be relevant to non-international armed conflicts.
2. The Rule is derived from Article 3 of the 1907 Hague Convention IV and Article 91 of AP/I.[5]

Rule 22

All those involved in the conduct of cyber operations, including attacks, are responsible for their respective roles and, commensurate with their involvement, have obligations to ensure that such operations are conducted in accordance with the applicable principles and rules of LOAC.

Commentary

1. The preceding Rule deals with State responsibility, whereas the present one addresses the issue of individual responsibility.
2. As for the general principle regarding individual responsibility, see Commentary to Rule 44.

Rule 23

(a) In the study, development, acquisition or adoption of a new cyber weapon, means or method of cyber warfare, a State that is party to Additional Protocol I must determine whether its employment would, in some or all circumstances, be prohibited by any rule of international law applicable to that State.

(b) In the acquisition of a new cyber weapon or means of cyber warfare, a State that is not party to Additional Protocol I should determine whether its employment would, in some or all circumstances, be prohibited by applicable principles and rules of LOAC.

Commentary

1. For the interpretation of this Rule, see the Commentary on Rule 7 which is applicable *mutatis mutandis*.
2. Due to the characteristics of cyber capabilities, the distinction between "a method of cyber warfare" and "means of cyber warfare" is still unclear.
3. Cyber capabilities in general are not inherently unlawful.
4. Cyber capabilities are so diverse and their effects so dependent on the circumstances (including the characteristics of the targeted system) that a legal review can likely only be conducted with regard to each individual capability. In most

[5]See chapter "Section I: Outer Space", fn. 13.

cases, legality will depend on *how* the capability is used rather than the capability itself.

Rule 24

In cyber operations occurring during an armed conflict, the concept of attack applies to all acts of violence against the adversary, whether in offence or defence. The acts must be intended to cause—or must be reasonably expected to result in—death, injury, destruction or damage. These acts generally do not include those intended to cause only temporary loss of functionality.

Commentary

1. For the interpretation of this Rule, see the Commentary on Rule 8 which is applicable *mutatis mutandis*.
2. This Rule applies in cyber operations as defined in Rule 20.
3. There are divergent views as to what constitutes damage in cyber warfare. One view is that damage must be limited specifically to a situation where it is physical and requires physical repairs. Another view is that extinguished or reduced functionality *per se*, irrespective of the need for physical repair, is sufficient.
4. The Group of Experts recognized that the notion of attack is based on the term "acts of violence". Such acts generally do not include cyber operations that merely result in the loss of functionality of cyber or related infrastructure, even though these operations are often colloquially described as "cyber attacks". Cyber operations that may be characterized as "violent", causing an intentional destruction of physical infrastructure or an intentional infliction of physical damage to property or injury to persons, would be attacks under this Rule.
5. The LOAC concept of "attack" has developed in the context of the infliction of physical destruction, damage, death or injury. However, cyber operations are liable to cause only non-physical destruction or damage, such as the deletion of data. Even if such effects are not characterized as destruction or damage, the respective acts could be subject to other LOAC rules, such as those relating to the protection of enemy property.
6. As for the temporary disruption of functionality of cyber or related infrastructure, it must be borne in mind that—although such disruption generally does not constitute an attack—it could be a component of an attack that is intended to cause death, injury, destruction or damage, for example through the crash of an aircraft.[6] Conversely, brief or minor disruption of Internet services or briefly disrupting, disabling, or interfering with communications, would generally not *per se* constitute an attack.

---

[6]*AMW Manual*, see chapter "Section I: Outer Space", fn. 1, see Commentary to Rule 1(e). Schmitt (ed.), *Tallinn Manual 2.0 on the International Law Applicable to Cyber Operations* (2nd ed.) (*Tallinn Manual*), (Cambridge: Cambridge University Press) (2017), see Rule 30.

Rule 25
In principle, cyber infrastructure belonging to the armed forces constitutes a military objective by nature.

Commentary
1. For military objectives by nature, see chapter "Section IX: Military Objectives by Nature".
2. The phrase "in principle" indicates that it is the general Rule subject to exceptions, such as in relation to medical installations and equipment.

Rule 26
Cyber infrastructure which does not belong to the armed forces—even if not constituting a military objective by nature—may still be attacked if it qualifies as a military objective by location, purpose or use. Cyber infrastructure not making an effective contribution to the enemy's military action is a civilian object and may therefore not be made the object of attack.

Commentary
1. The Group of Experts agreed that, at present, the reference to "location" seemed to have uncertain factual relevance to cyber warfare. Therefore, this Rule is mainly directed at use or purpose (with an understanding that purpose is related to intended future use).
2. For an object to be classified as a military objective, any one of the grounds specified (nature, location, purpose or use) will suffice. As long as the military objective is defined by any one of the grounds, no other ground is required for consideration.
3. Cyber infrastructure that is not classified as a military objective is by definition a civilian object and thus protected from being made the object of attack.

Rule 27
The concept of direct participation in hostilities applies to civilians, including civilian employees of State agencies, who conduct cyber operations in the context of an armed conflict.

Commentary
1. For general remarks on the concept of direct participation in hostilities, see chapter "Section VII: Civilians Directly Participating in Hostilities".
2. This Rule has a generalised applicability, not only to civilians who act individually or collectively but also to those employed by State agencies. Some States seem to be under the impression that civilian employees of State agencies are not subject to the general Rule relating to DPH. The Group of Experts believed that it needed to be made clear that DPH applies to all civilians without exception relating to their employment.

Rule 28
Cyber operations qualifying as direct participation in hostilities may include:

(a) Any cyber activity designed or intended to directly cause death, injury, damage or destruction to an adverse party;
(b) Cyber defence of military objectives against enemy attacks;
(c) Contributing to targeting procedures, such as helping to identify or prioritize targets;
(d) Engaging in planning specific cyber attacks; or
(e) Providing or relaying information of tactical relevance for the purpose of aiding in combat operations.

Commentary
1. The overall definition of activities amounting to direct participation in hostilities is highly controversial. However, the Group of Experts agreed on the five categories of activities identified in this Rule, without prejudice to other activities regarding which no consensus could be reached.
2. See also paragraph 1 of the Commentary to Rule 13 with regard to activities amounting to DPH.
3. As for paragraph (e) of this Rule, it should be noted that obtaining military intelligence as such is not sufficient to qualify as DPH. Conversely, providing or relaying such information of tactical relevance for the purpose of aiding in combat operations is undoubtedly considered DPH. There is a borderline issue of the processing of information, where the Group of Experts could not determine whether such activity is sufficient to qualify as DPH.
4. In view of the severe consequences of DPH the decision on whether an activity qualifies as DPH should be based on reasonably reliable information.
5. See also chapters "Section VII: Civilians Directly Participating in Hostilities" and "Section VIII: Civilians Participating in Unmanned Operations".

Rule 29
In cyber operations constituting attacks, feasible precautions should be taken where necessary in order to avoid, or in any event minimize, destruction or damage to civilian objects, or death or injury to civilians.

Commentary
1. The reference to "feasible precautions" here parallels Rule 14. The meaning of the phrase is defined in the Commentary to that Rule.
2. Taking feasible precautions will only be required when the operation constitutes an attack. See Rule 24.
3. For the purposes of taking feasible precautions, it may be necessary to collect information about the architecture of the network or operating system that is to be

attacked. The assessment of potential or likely collateral damage will largely depend on the characteristics of the targeted system.

4. To identify whether the target is a military objective and to assess the expected collateral damage, Parties conducting cyber operations should, if feasible, collect sufficiently accurate information about the architecture of the enemy's network or the relevant operating system.[7]
5. Because of the technicalities of cyber operations, the reasonable military commander will almost inevitably need assistance from cyber experts in order to determine the potential or likely incidental civilian damage of a cyber attack, unless he or she is a trained cyber expert himself/herself.

Rule 30

A Belligerent State should not conduct cyber operations that constitute attacks causing physical damage to or destruction of objects located in neutral territory, including neutral cyber infrastructure, unless the Neutral State is unable or unwilling to terminate an abuse of such objects or infrastructure by an adversary of the Belligerent State.

Commentary

1. The meaning of "attacks" in cyber warfare is explained in Rule 24 and Commentary.
2. It is unclear whether and to what extent the law of neutrality applies in the cyber context. Divergent views exists with respect to this question. Some States believe that the *raison d'être* of the law of neutrality, and its reliance on the concept of neutral territory, is inconsistent with the characteristics of cyber activities. Others, on the other hand, argue that the law of neutrality may be applied in the cyber context *mutatis mutandis*.
3. Accordingly, and since the Group of Experts recognized that there was not sufficient acknowledged State practice and *opinio juris* as regards cyber operations related to armed conflict, it was decided to avoid the use of mandatory language in the present Rule (such as "must" or "shall") and instead to use "should" in the elaboration of this Rule.
4. This Rule is based on the principles of customary law governing neutrality, as expressed in the 1907 Hague Convention V on Neutral Powers and Persons in War on Land.[8]
5. The inviolability of neutral territory means that Belligerent States should not conduct cyber operations constituting attacks against targets therein, regardless of their governmental or private character. As for the mere routing of data through neutral cyber infrastructure (including the Internet), see Rule 33 and accompanying Commentary.

---

[7] *Tallinn Manual,* see fn. 6, Rule 53.

[8] See chapter "Section I: Outer Space", fn. 23, Articles 1 and 2.

6. Equally protected is cyber infrastructure that belongs to a Belligerent State although located in the territory of a Neutral State, provided that it is not being abused in support of the military activities of an adversary Belligerent State.
7. The Rule does not apply to espionage. Likewise, it does not apply to dissemination of propaganda or other activities that are not intended—or are not reasonably expected—to cause death, injury, destruction or damage.
8. Cyber operations merely causing inconvenience (as distinct from death, injury, destruction or damage) are not covered by this Rule.
9. In case of an abuse by a Belligerent State of objects or infrastructure located in neutral territory, cyber operations against the Neutral State amounting to use of force under the Charter of the United Nations Article 2(4) will be lawful only if they are consistent with the inherent right to self-defence (as recognized by Article 51 of the Charter) or when authorized by the Security Council.[9]
10. The foregoing Commentary is without prejudice to the legality of an extraterritorial exercise of the right of self-defence against non-state actors located in and operating from the territory of a Neutral State.

Rule 31
Belligerent States must not launch attacks from cyber infrastructure located in neutral territory or under the exclusive control of Neutral States.

Commentary

1. See Commentary to Rule 30.
2. The launching by a Belligerent State of attacks from neutral infrastructure against an enemy is a violation of the territorial sovereignty of the Neutral State. The Group of Experts was aware of the technical and other difficulties of definitively identifying the actual source of a cyber attack. Despite these difficulties, they took the position that the principle of the inviolability of neutral territory applies to the launching of a cyber attack. They further recognized that technology is evolving rapidly, such that the interpretation of what constitutes "launching" for these purposes is likely to be affected in the future.
3. In light of the interconnected nature of cyberspace (including the Internet), and the degree to which cyber infrastructure in one country is used in other countries, the Group of Experts considered that it—in view of the current extent of State practice—would impossible to apply the prohibition reflected in this Rule to cyber operations not constituting attacks. As for the meaning of "attacks", see Rule 24. For the mere routing of data through neutral cyber infrastructure, see Rule 33.

[9] See chapter "Section I: Outer Space", fn. 5.

4. The prohibition applies to both public and private cyber infrastructure located within neutral territory (including civilian cyber infrastructure owned by a Belligerent Party to the conflict or its nationals), and to neutral non-commercial governmental cyber infrastructure (under the exclusive control of the State) irrespective of its location.[10] Both the remote taking control of computer systems located in neutral territory to conduct cyber operations that constitute attacks and the execution of cyber operations that constitute attacks by organs or agents of the Belligerent State located in the territory of the Neutral State are prohibited.[11]
5. In the case of botnets used to conduct attacks, the prohibition relates to the situation in which the botmaster controls a botnet from neutral territory.

Rule 32
If in the context of an armed conflict a Belligerent Party undertakes cyber operations constituting an attack from cyber infrastructure located on Neutral territory, the neutral State must use reasonable means at its disposal to terminate the attack once it becomes aware of it.

Commentary

1. This Rule is based on the principles of customary law of neutrality, as expressed in the 1907 Hague Convention V on Neutral Powers and Persons in War on Land and the 1907 Hague Convention XIII on Neutrality in Naval War.[12]
2. The duty to use reasonable means to terminate on-going cyber attacks hinges on knowledge by the Neutral State as to the use of cyber infrastructure within its territory. Such knowledge may be based either on information obtained by the Neutral State itself or on information provided to it, including by the aggrieved Belligerent State.
3. Assuming that such knowledge exists, the Neutral State must take reasonable action to terminate the cyber attacks by the Belligerent State. However, the Neutral State may not be able to prevent such attacks before they are launched. The Neutral State has no duty continuously to monitor cyber traffic within its territory.
4. The duty to use all reasonable means to terminate attacks applies to cyber attacks launched by botmasters located in neutral territory.

---

[10] *Tallinn Manual,* see fn. 6, page 248, and 1907 Hague Convention (XIII) on Neutrality in Naval War, see chapter "Section I: Outer Space", fn. 23, Articles 8 and 25.

[11] *Tallinn Manual,* see fn. 6, page 251.

[12] 1907 Hague Convention (V) on Neutral Powers and Persons in Case of War on Land, see chapter "Section I: Outer Space", fn. 23, Article 5. 1907 Hague Convention (XIII) on Neutrality in Naval War, see fn. 25, Article 8.

Rule 33

The mere fact that cyber operations are routed through neutral cyber infrastructure does not constitute a violation of neutrality.

Commentary

1. The Group of Experts acknowledged that the routing of cyber operations will, likely, involve the dynamic relocation of individual packages through diverse servers.
2. The fact that particular packages might move through neutral cyber infrastructure (including the Internet) would not, *per se*, amount to a breach of neutrality.

Rule 34

(a) Without prejudice to Rule 32, the mere use of neutral cyber infrastructure by a Belligerent State is not generally prohibited.

Commentary

1. This Rule is based on Article 8 of the 1907 Hague Convention V on Neutral Powers and Persons in War on Land.[13]
2. Rule 32, to which this Rule is subordinated, excludes cyber attacks.

(b) Belligerent States are thus permitted to:

i. Erect a new cyber communication installation on the territory of a Neutral State that is exclusively used for non-military communications;
ii. Use an existing cyber communication installation established by them before the outbreak of the armed conflict (including for military communications), provided that it is open for the service of public messages; or
iii. Use an existing cyber communication installation established by them before the outbreak of the armed conflict and which is not open for the service of public messages, provided it is for non-military communications.

Commentary

1. This Rule is linked to Article 3 of the 1907 Hague Convention V. The expression "for the service of public messages" is found in Article 3(b).[14]
2. Cyber communication installations may include computers, servers, routers and networks.

[13] See chapter "Section I: Outer Space", fn. 23.

[14] *Ibid.*

Rule 35

Any measure of restriction or prohibition taken by a Neutral State with regard to the activities referred to in Rule 34 should be impartially applied to all Belligerent States.

Commentary

1. This Rule is based on Article 9 of the Hague Convention V on Neutral Powers in War on Land.[15]

[15] *Ibid.*

Section III: Remote and Autonomous Weapons

1. The technologies discussed in this Section are either novel or have yet to emerge and are not explicitly dealt with in either customary international law or in treaty law. The principal purpose of the present Section is to explain some of the main legal issues that the development of these new technologies seem likely to raise in relation to LOAC.
2. Different countries may choose to categorize these technologies in differing terms. This variety could not be adequately reflected in the present Section. Moreover, the terminology and definitions used in this Section may be expected to evolve in the light of future developments. Accordingly, the phrase "For the purposes of this Manual" (appearing in Rule 36 and other provisions of this Section) reflects the provisional status of the language that is employed.
3. The implementation of the law of targeting under LOAC is traditionally achieved by the human user of a weapon system applying the principle of distinction and the rules as to discrimination, proportionality and precautions. A number of the technologies discussed in the present Section may, in the future, enable a weapon system to make determinations as to whether an attack will take place and if so what the target will be and how the attack will be prosecuted. Even when the technologies covered by this Section are employed, the role of a human user of a weapon system may not be excluded. However, if no human being will play a role in the attack decision-making process, the question will arise as to whether some other method can be adopted to enable application of the principle of distinction and the rules pertaining to discrimination, proportionality and precautions. It was the position of the Group of Experts that, irrespective of the method of warfare adopted, the aforementioned principle and rules must be observed.
4. It should be emphasized that LOAC does not impose obligations on weapon systems themselves, but rather on the persons making decisions in connection with their use. In other words, LOAC requires that those persons will only act in compliance with LOAC principles and rules (taking into account the systems

Y. Dinstein, A. W. Dahl, *Oslo Manual on Select Topics of the Law of Armed Conflict*,
https://doi.org/10.1007/978-3-030-39169-0_3

capabilities and constraints). In the final analysis, legal responsibility will devolve on the State and on individuals involved in that activity (see Rules 43 and 44).

Rule 36
For the purposes of this Manual, a "remotely piloted aircraft" (RPA) is an aircraft that is controlled via a remote communication link by a human operator who is not located on board the aircraft.

Commentary

1. The term "remotely piloted aircraft" (RPA) has been used to reflect that the aircraft is piloted by an individual who is not on board. The word "drones" is also frequently used to refer to such vehicles. The controller of an RPA may occupy a control station distant from the RPA's area of operation. From that control station the controller employs computerized links with the RPA to guide it and monitors the output of its sensors.
2. RPAs are aircraft and are distinguished from other aerial weapon systems such as missiles. In contrast to missiles, RPAs are normally recoverable.
3. The AMW Manual draws a distinction between "unmanned aerial vehicles" in general and "unmanned combat aerial vehicles", the latter comprising unmanned military aircraft of any size that can carry and launch a weapon or that can use on-board technology to direct a weapon to a target.[1] The term RPA, however, does not distinguish between unmanned aircraft on the basis of their roles, which may include, e.g., reconnaissance, surveillance, information gathering, communications or other battle support, logistical or general military tasks and attacks.
4. RPAs can vary in size, e.g., from Global Hawk with a wingspan of 116 feet and a payload of up to 2000 pounds to the US Defense Advanced Research Projects Agency Nano Air Vehicle with a wingspan of 16 cm and a weight of 19 g. Both would, however, constitute aircraft,[2] and thus (if remotely controlled), RPAs.
5. RPAs using currently available technology, whether they are being employed on reconnaissance, surveillance, attack or other missions, are normally recovered at the conclusion of the assigned mission. However, the issue of recovery is not essential in terms of the definition of RPAs. The essential features of an RPA are that (i) it is piloted by a person who is not on board the aircraft and (ii) being an aircraft, it derives lift from the air. The possibility cannot be excluded that disposable RPAs may be developed. If such disposable systems derive lift from the air and are remotely piloted, they could, for the purposes of this Manual, be classed as RPAs.

---

[1] *AMW Manual*, see fn. 1, rules 1(dd) and 1(ee).

[2] UK Ministry of Defence, *The Manual of the Law of Armed Conflict* (*UK Manual*), Oxford: Oxford University Press (2004), paragraph 12.4.1 as amended.

6. During an international armed conflict, an RPA may only be used to exercise belligerent rights, such as attack or interception operations, if it fulfills the requirements of a military aircraft.[3] To qualify as a military aircraft, it must be operated by the armed forces of a State, bear the military markings of that State (provided the size of the aircraft allows for such marking), be commanded by a member of the armed forces and be controlled by personnel subject to regular armed forces discipline.[4]

Rule 37

For the purposes of this Manual, a "highly automated" weapon system is a system that, once activated, is capable of identifying and engaging a target without further human input, while being constrained by algorithms that determine its responses by imposing rules of engagement and setting mission parameters which limit its ability to act independently.

Commentary

1. A "highly automated" weapon system performs functions in a self-contained and independent manner once activated. It independently verifies or detects a particular type of target and then fires or detonates a munition. Automated technologies in general are not new and have been employed in the past, e.g., in mines and booby-traps.[5]
2. Reference is being made here to "highly automated" as distinct from "automated" in recognition that there are numerous degrees of automation and a variety of functions that are capable of being automated. These may include, e.g., navigation of a platform; navigation of a munition; the co-ordination or fusion of data with a view to presentation of it to a pilot or other operator; functions associated with the fusing of the weapon, the locking on by an air to air missile to a target aircraft to which it has been directed by a pilot; and so on. Numerous weapon systems incorporate automated functions but do not come within the definition of autonomous systems, see Rule 38.

---

[3] Hague Rules Concerning the Control of Wireless Telegraphy in Time of War and Air Warfare (Hague Draft Rules of Aerial Warfare) (1923), *Laws of Armed Conflicts*, at page 315, Article 13; *UK Manual*, see fn. 2, para 12.34; German Federal Ministry of Defence, Law of Armed Conflict Manual (*German Manual*) (2013), Joint Service Regulation (ZDv) 15/2, para 1103; *US DoD Manual*, see chapter "Section II: Cyber Operations", fn. 4, para 14.3.3.

[4] Hague Draft Rules of Aerial Warfare 1923, Articles 3, 13 and 16, see fn. 3; and *US DoD Manual*, see chapter "Section II: Cyber Operations", fn. 4, paras 14.3.2 and 14.3.3; so, law enforcement, customs, or coastguard aircraft, including RPA, that do not qualify as military aircraft and that are not incorporated into the armed forces may not engage in hostilities. It remains to be seen whether, as small and unmanned military air platforms start to be more widely used, States continue to apply to them rules as to military and nationality marking.

[5] *US DoD Manual*, see chapter "Section II: Cyber Operations", fn. 4, para 6.5.9.1.

Rule 38
For the purposes of this Manual, an "autonomous" weapon system is a weapon system that is programmed to apply human-like reasoning to determine whether an object or person is a target, whether it should be attacked, and if so, how and when.

Commentary

1. The concept of autonomy as used here may be narrower than that used by some roboticists.
2. There are different definitions of "autonomous weapon systems". For example, the US Department of Defense Directive 3000.09 defines "autonomous weapon systems" as "a weapon system that, once activated, can select and engage targets without further intervention by a human operator. This includes human-supervised autonomous weapon systems that are designed to allow human operators to override operation of the weapon system, but can select and engage targets without further human input after activation." In this Manual systems described in the second sentence of the US definition come within the ambit of Rule 39 (b), *i.e.,* "man-on-the-loop systems".
3. This Rule reflects that the single most important defining characteristic of an autonomous system is its ability to apply what perhaps can most accurately be described as "human-like reasoning". By using this term, the Group of Experts was seeking to express the process of human judgment in which disparate facts are assessed and sometimes compared in order to reach an evaluative decision which will require the application of judgment. At the present time, such systems are not known to exist.
4. It is the application of human-like reasoning independently to identify and decide to engage targets that is the vital distinguishing feature of this technology. Such a weapon system is not pre-programmed to target a specified object or person. It is the software that decides which target to engage, how and when. Accordingly, the weapon system is making the relevant judgments by applying the kinds of thought process that a human being would use when employing a more conventional weapon system, and, again like a human decision-maker, the autonomous weapon system has the capacity to adapt its behaviour in response to changed circumstances.
5. The reference to being "programmed" in the definition indicates that the system's software will have been so engineered as to enable, perhaps require, the system to analyze information and make decisions having applied human-like reasoning to the facts that either it detects or that are otherwise disclosed to the system. The reasoning process is likely to be similar, in terms of decisions made, to that which a human being might be expected to undertake, although the logical processes may not necessarily be the same as a human being would apply.

6. While it is possible to characterize an autonomous weapon system as making a decision in a factual sense, it is also critical to emphasize that LOAC imposes obligations on persons and does not impose direct obligations on the weapons themselves. LOAC does not, for example, express a requirement that an autonomous weapon system must determine whether its target is a military objective, if no human being is involved in the attack decision-making process. Nevertheless, LOAC still requires the attack to be conducted in accordance with targeting law (see Rule 41). For State responsibility and any responsibility by individuals involved in an attack, see Rules 43 and 44.

Rule 39
For the purposes of this Manual:

(a) A "man-in-the-loop system" positions the operator within the loop formed by the decision-making process of the system such that the human operator decides on the firing of a weapon.

Commentary

1. The cycle of receiving input, analyzing the input and taking action can be regarded as a loop, and the presence of the human controller within this loop characterizes the system as "man-in-the-loop". A "man-in-the-loop system" positions the operator within the loop formed by the decision-making process of the system, using up- and down-links to the remotely piloted aircraft.
2. Up- and down-links are the means whereby the human operator communicates with the vehicle and whereby the operator receives communications from the vehicle.
3. Where RPAs are concerned, the link from the controller to the RPA (see Rule 36) is used, *inter alia*, to direct the flight of the RPA and to instruct the RPA to perform tasks. The link down from the RPA to the control station is used, *inter alia*, to deliver information from on-board sensors. Taken together, these links can be regarded as a loop, and the presence of the controller within this loop characterizes such systems as "man-in-the-loop systems".
4. Remotely controlled vehicles in other environments may have similar capabilities for the receipt and transmission of data.

(b) A "man-on-the-loop system" is one that is capable of highly automated or autonomous operation but is supervised by a human operator who has the capability to intervene and override a decision, such as the decision to fire a weapon.

Commentary

1. A "man-on-the-loop system" is differently configured from a "man-in-the-loop system". The operator is not positioned, either physically or structurally, within the loop formed by the system's decision-making process to fire a weapon after receiving external inputs. The weapon system may be capable of making and

implementing its own determinations as to attack, reconnaissance, information gathering or other tasks, but the "man-on-the-loop" element inserts the presence of a human operator who—while not involved in the firing of the weapon or other decisions—is nevertheless able to observe the determination being made and the action being taken by the weapon system and to intervene and countermand any determination or actions that seems likely to lead to unlawful or undesirable consequences. Such aircraft can be distinguished from other aircraft in which the human controller decides which target is to be engaged or which task is to be undertaken and who undertakes the attack by initiating the firing mechanism or transmitting the instructions for the performance of the chosen task using the remote-control facility built into the RPA system.

2. The use of a "man-on-the-loop system" for the gathering of information, for reconnaissance or similar tasks, could assist in addressing issues under the law of targeting. Indeed, using such systems to obtain timely, accurate information as to the situation in an area where attacks are intended is likely to promote adherence to the principle of distinction. There is no LOAC rule prohibiting or limiting the use of such technologies. Furthermore, such systems will generally be equipped with sensors and associated systems that are designed to allow military commanders to control the effects of these weapons (e.g., to ensure that the weapons do not cause excessive collateral damage or result in "friendly fire").
3. The human being who is monitoring a "man-on-the-loop" system and who is able to cancel a firing determination that the system might undertake, may assist in ensuring that the system can be used in accordance with LOAC. This is not intended to imply that LOAC requires that a person must necessarily be in or on the loop to render the use of a highly automated or autonomous system lawful. If the highly automated or autonomous system is capable of being used in accordance with targeting law, LOAC contains no specific requirement that a person be either in or on the loop in the sense that those terms are employed in this Manual. Rather, where necessary, the monitoring can be conducive to avoiding or minimizing the risk of civilian casualties.
4. The person "on-the-loop" may find it necessary to intervene and countermand any determination made by the weapon system for a variety of reasons. So, for example, there could be clear cases in which (if the weapon were to fire) a civilian taking no direct part in the hostilities, or a civilian object, would be struck, and the "man-on-the-loop" would be obliged to intervene and stop the weapon system.[6] There are other circumstances when such intervention would be called for, for example if the object of attack is a person or object entitled to special protection under the law of armed conflict, or if the attack that the weapon system has decided upon would be contrary to the commander's intent.

[6] AP/I, see chapter "Section I: Outer Space", fn. 13, Articles 51(2), 52(1) and 57(2)(b).

5. While the presence of the person "on-the-loop" may, in the context of a particular weapon system, be the aspect that enables the required precautions in attack to be undertaken, the circumstances in which the person is operating "on-the-loop" will determine whether the precautions are actually taken with sufficient care. Thus, for example, if a person is contemporaneously placed "on-the-loop" of numerous weapon systems, or of weapon systems undertaking numerous contemporaneous operations or attacks so that he/she is not practically able to monitor properly the precautions that targeting law requires (including those referred to in the present Commentary) this might have the consequence that the requirement to take feasible precautions would not be complied with to an acceptable degree. The word "might" is used here because there may be other elements of the weapon system or of its method of operation that do enable particular precautions to be taken. The point remains, however, that if legal compliance relies on a man "on-the-loop" and if that person is over-tasked in whatever way, compliance is put at risk.

Rule 40
For the purposes of this Manual, a "swarm" is a group of aircraft or other vehicles of any size that is performing (or is intended to perform) military tasks in which the individual aircraft or other vehicles are autonomously coordinating or acting in formation.

Commentary

1. Given the early state of "swarming" technology, it is unclear what could arise in the context of aircraft being operated as part of a "swarm" for the performance of military tasks. Swarms could comprise numerous aircraft and whether the individual vehicles of the swarm are large or small or of various sizes might not be relevant to the characterization of the group as a swarm. It is possible that some swarms will operate such that the individual members maintain a fixed formation while other swarms may involve dissimilar movements. Swarms could involve RPAs, highly automated systems or autonomous systems. Other swarms may comprise a mixture of these types of platforms, or the same platforms may have different modes of operation.
2. Whether operating in formation or with the individual vehicles undertaking dissimilar movements, the swarm will need to maintain some form of coordination among its vehicles to avoid collisions and other mutual interference.
3. What appears distinctive regarding "swarms" is the use of autonomy to coordinate vehicles in the swarm by, for example, distributing tasks among vehicles in the swarm.

Rule 41
The employment of remotely piloted, highly automated or autonomous systems and swarms for the purposes of attack is subject to the applicable

principles and rules of LOAC, in particular distinction, proportionality and the obligation to take feasible precautions.

Commentary

1. The Group of Experts agreed that the existing principles and rules of LOAC are the basis on which the lawfulness of using RPAs, highly automated or autonomous weapon systems, or swarms is to be judged.
2. For the notion of "applicable principles and rules of LOAC", see paragraph 4 of the Commentary to Rule 2.
3. Human-like reasoning (referred to in Rule 38) may not be necessary to secure compliance with targeting law by an autonomous weapon system in specific circumstances. For instance, the employment of a weapon system may be limited to a time and location where all those present certainly qualify as lawful targets.
4. In other situations, it would be necessary to ensure that the introduction of an autonomous weapon system operating with human-like reasoning would be in full compliance with the principles and rules of LOAC. This could be attained if the weapon system were able to make two classes of determination. The first concerns the lawfulness of the target, *i.e.* a determination whether it is a combatant, a civilian taking a direct part in the hostilities or an object that is a military objective. The second concerns the legality of attacking it in the circumstances prevailing at the time.
5. It should be stressed that RPAs, autonomous weapons systems and "swarms" are not per se prohibited by the principles and rules of LOAC.
6. If a swarm is used to undertake reconnaissance, information gathering or other tasks that do not constitute part of an attack, LOAC issues will not be engaged merely by virtue of the character of the group of aircraft so involved as a swarm.
7. If a swarm is being used to undertake attacks, the factors that determine whether and to what extent controllers or operators are required may include: (i) the number of aircraft in the swarm; (ii) the number, nature and circumstances of the targets that are to be attacked; (iii) the nature, quality and reliability of the up- and down-links to each aircraft; and (iv) the degree to which the swarm is operated in a formation.
8. If achieving compliance with the applicable principles and rules of LOAC necessitates human presence "in" or "on-the-loop", it is important to ensure that the relevant personnel are not tasked to such a degree or located in such a way as to preclude their proper performance of the required feasible precautions. If the technology incorporated into the swarm is such that the individual weapon systems are capable of making the determinations required by targeting law in the intended circumstances of use, the presence of a person or persons "in" or "on the loop" of elements of the swarm may not be required. It will be a question of fact whether the swarm does indeed have that technical capability and whether it is able to operate with an acceptable level of reliability. In certain circumstances,

achieving compliance with targeting law may require that there be sufficient controllers or operators adequately linked in with the activities of each aircraft.

9. The determination whether or not to act in formation may be taken autonomously.

Rule 42

(a) In the study, development, acquisition or adoption of new weapon systems addressed in this Section, a State that is party to Additional Protocol I must determine whether its employment would, in some or all circumstances, be prohibited by any rule of international law applicable to that State.

(b) In the acquisition of a new weapon system addressed in this Section, a State that is not party to Additional Protocol I should determine whether its employment would, in some or all circumstances, be prohibited by applicable principles and rules of LOAC.

Commentary

1. For the interpretation of this Rule, see the Commentary on Rule 7 which is applicable *mutatis mutandis*.
2. There are at present no rules of LOAC that specifically refer to RPAs or other remotely piloted or controlled weapon platforms. Similarly, no specific rules refer to highly automated or autonomous attack technologies as such.[7] The fact that a weapon system is remotely controlled, highly automated or autonomous does not, therefore, *per se* render the system unlawful.
3. When the review concerns such weapon systems, it is necessary for the person conducting the weapon review to determine whether the weapon system is capable of being used in accordance with the rules prescribed by LOAC. The question is not whether the weapon system will comply with targeting law on a particular occasion but whether the way in which the system is designed and will be operated enables the targeting law rules to be properly applied. In practice, the main question may be whether the anticipated employment of the weapon system will be consistent with the principles of distinction and proportionality.

Rule 43

With respect to an armed conflict, States bear responsibility for internationally wrongful operations using RPAs, highly automated weapon systems or autonomous weapons that are attributable to them. Such responsibility encompasses actions by all persons belonging to the armed forces.

---

[7]Note, however, that Protocol (II) to the Conventional Weapons Convention on Prohibitions or Restrictions on the Use of Mines, Booby-Traps and Other Devices (Protocol II to CCW) (1980), *The Laws of Armed Conflicts*, page 185, address, inter alia, "other devices" which include manually emplaced munitions actuated by remote control.

Commentary

1. For an interpretation of this Rule, see the commentaries on Rules 5 and 21.

Rule 44

All those involved in the conduct of operations, including attacks, using RPAs, highly automated weapon systems or autonomous weapons, are responsible for their respective roles and, commensurate with their involvement, have obligations to ensure that such operations are conducted in accordance with the applicable principles and rules of LOAC.

Commentary

1. See Commentary on Rules 5 and 22.
2. Numerous individuals may have various roles that may be relevant to the conduct of an RPA operation. Those individuals include, but are not limited to: (i) the RPA operator; (ii) any technicians who may be assisting the operator; (iii) those involved in launching the RPA; (iv) the commander of the mission; (v) those who planned the mission; (vi) those who prepared the software; (vii) those who loaded data into the mission control systems; (viii) those who gave legal advice in connection with the mission and so on. All such individuals have obligations with respect to the implementation of applicable principles and rules of LOAC.
3. The degree and nature of the responsibility of each individual depends, *inter alia*, on the nature and extent of that individual's role, on the rank of the individual, on the operational relationships between the persons involved, and on the information available to the particular individual at a specific time. Although the negligent performance of duties is likely to attract disciplinary liability for armed forces members under their service code, gross negligence, recklessness and intent may, depending on the consequences, involve criminal liability.
4. Manning and other arrangements for RPA operations should facilitate compliance with targeting law.
5. The information that the sensors aboard an RPA gather may be used to support the decision to engage a specific target, may be used in support of other military operations or may contribute more generally to the commander's picture of the battlespace. An RPA that is on a reconnaissance or information gathering mission will generally be used to provide information for one or more of these purposes.
6. The mere fact that an autonomous or highly automated weapon system is used to undertake an attack does not preclude the potential liability under international criminal law of any person for his/her involvement in such a military operation.

7. In view of the novelty and complexity of the technology, it is not clear exactly where responsibility under international criminal law will lie for specific acts performed by an autonomous or highly automated weapon system. See chapter "Section XVII: International Criminal Law" with regard to individual criminal liability in international law and command responsibility particularly.

Rule 45
A person who wrests control of a weapon system referred to in this Section assumes responsibility for its subsequent use in accordance with the degree and the duration of the control exercised.

Commentary

1. This Rule refers to the individual responsibility of a person who wrests control of weapon systems referred to in this Section. Should such a person act on behalf of a State, his/her wrongful act will be attributable to that State which will bear State responsibility, see Rule 43.
2. This Rule reflects that a cyber hacker who achieves control of the enemy's weapon system or its munition becomes responsible for his/her subsequent employment of the weapon. The hacker's employment of the weapon must comply with principles and rules of LOAC including distinction, discrimination[8] and proportionality as well as the obligation to take precautions in attack. If the cyber hacker does not achieve absolute control of the weapon system and its munitions, but interferes in the way in which the weapon system and munitions are operated by the enemy, responsibility for the use of the weapon system or munition should be determined in accordance with the following criteria.

   a. If a cyber hacker exercises control of a weapon system referred to in this Section and knowingly or intentionally directs its weapon—or knowingly or intentionally causes the weapon system to direct weapons—at a target or category of targets of his/her choice, he/she becomes responsible for the consequences of such employment of the weapon.
   b. This subparagraph applies if the cyber hacker does this with the intention of causing the weapon to attack civilians, civilian objects or persons or objects entitled to specific protection, or to undertake indiscriminate attacks. If this sub-paragraph applies, the cyber hacker is responsible for the consequences of the use of the weapon.
   c. If in the circumstances described in sub-paragraph b the cyber operation foreseeably causes the adverse party's attack(s) to become indiscriminate,

[8]Discrimination is here used to refer to indiscriminate attacks.

the cyber operation is likely (depending on the circumstances) to conflict with obligations under Articles 57(1) and 58(c) of AP/I.[9]

3. If two adversaries are contesting control over a weapon system and the system ends up crashing and harming civilians, responsibility may be impossible to attribute to either of them.

[9] See chapter "Section I: Outer Space", fn. 13.

Section IV: Unmanned Maritime Systems

To a certain extent, this Section overlaps some provisions of chapter "Section III: Remote and Autonomous Weapons" inasmuch as both Sections deal with unmanned systems. However, whereas chapter "Section III: Remote and Autonomous Weapons" addresses both unmanned platforms and weapon systems, the present Section focuses on unmanned maritime platforms that may or may not be integral parts of a weapon system. The maritime platforms and systems dealt with here must therefore be distinguished from automated weapon systems, in particular those for the defence of surface platforms against missile threats. Accordingly, the terminology used in this Section does not necessarily replicate that used in chapter "Section III: Remote and Autonomous Weapons".

Rule 46

(a) "Unmanned Maritime Systems" (UMS) are:

i. self-propelled or remotely-navigated craft that are normally recoverable and designed to perform functions at sea by operating on the surface, semi-submerged or undersea; and

ii. either:

a. are remotely operated,

b. are remotely controlled, or

c. perform their functions independently from a human controller or operator on board the craft.

Commentary

1. UMS comprise surface, semi-submersible and undersea vehicles of various sizes. They are either remotely operated/controlled or "autonomous". Many of the systems in use today are remotely operated or controlled but they "capitalize on automation in extreme circumstances, such as a lost link condition, to perform automatically a pre-programmed set of instructions." At present, there is no

Y. Dinstein, A. W. Dahl, *Oslo Manual on Select Topics of the Law of Armed Conflict*,
https://doi.org/10.1007/978-3-030-39169-0_4

maritime system which may be considered as fully autonomous as defined in Rule 38.

2. UMS can perform a wide variety of missions or tasks. It is important to bear in mind that UMS, in particular Unmanned Underwater Vehicles (UUVs), are today used for the performance of the following important civilian/non-military tasks:

   a. Offshore oil and gas missions;
   b. Undersea cable deployment and inspection;
   c. Commercial salvage;
   d. Aquaculture; and
   e. Science missions, such as oceanography and marine archaeology.

3. According to the DoD Roadmap, current military missions performed by UMS, *i.e.* Unmanned Surface Vehicles (USVs) and UUVs, include "mine warfare, mine neutralization, reconnaissance, surveillance, hydrographic surveying, environmental analysis, special operations, and oceanographic research". Similarly, the UUV Master Plan identifies nine specific mission categories and prioritizes them as follows:

   a. Intelligence, surveillance, and reconnaissance (ISR);
   b. Mine countermeasures (MCM);
   c. Anti-submarine Warfare (ASW);
   d. Inspection/identification;
   e. Oceanography;
   f. Communication/navigation network node (CN^3);
   g. Payload delivery;
   h. Information operations (IO); and
   i. Time-critical strike (TCS).

4. Although it is still possible to distinguish between remotely operated and autonomous maritime vehicles, certain vehicles may have technological capabilities to be operated either by remote control or autonomously.

(b) UMS include Unmanned Surface Vehicles (USVs) and Unmanned Underwater Vehicles (UUVs).

Commentary

1. According to the US DoD, "UMS comprise unmanned maritime vehicles (UMVs), which include both unmanned surface vehicles (USVs) and unmanned undersea vehicles (UUVs), all necessary support components, and the fully integrated sensors and payloads necessary to accomplish the required missions".[1]

---

[1]U.S. Department of Defense, *Unmanned Systems Integrated Roadmap FY2013-2038* (*DoD Roadmap*), page 8.

Although those definitions seem to suggest that UMVs/USVs are but components of UMS, it would not be correct to hold that UMVs/USVs do not qualify as "systems" because they are composed of various subsystems.[2]

2. While some Governments presently prefer the use of the term "UMV", the Group of Experts took note of the fact that there is not yet a sufficiently agreed upon understanding of the various concepts. Although it is possible that all UMVs will be considered "vessels" or "ships", State practice has not yet crystallized. Since a distinction between "systems" and "vehicles" does not prove helpful, it seems appropriate, for the purposes of this Manual, to consider the terms "UMS" and "UMV" as synonymous.

Rule 47

If owned or operated by a State and used only on Government non-commercial service, all UMS enjoy sovereign immunity. This is without prejudice to their status under LOAC.

Commentary

1. The language of this Rule is based on Article 96 of the United Nations Convention on the Law of the Sea (UNCLOS).[3]
2. Nevertheless, although UMS navigate at sea, it is not clear whether they can be considered ships. The international law of the sea lacks a uniform definition of the term "ship". UNCLOS uses the terms "vessel" and "ship" interchangeably, without providing a definition of either term. Other relevant treaties provide varying definitions that are functionally limited. While those treaties generally do not prohibit treating UMS as vessels or ships, a number of the relevant rules were created specifically with manned systems in mind. In view of these difficulties, UMS are in some contexts not characterized as ships or vessels but rather as "craft".[4] It is quite possible that a considerable number of States are not prepared to recognize UMS as ships/vessels, although more may be known about State views in the coming years given efforts at the International Maritime Organization (IMO) to assimilate unmanned craft to vessels/ships.
3. If UMS are operated by the armed forces or any other Government agency of a State, they may not necessarily qualify as warships or State ships. However, since they either constitute State property or used only on Government non-commercial service,

[2]For example, the major UUV's subsystems are: the pressure hull, the hydrodynamic hull, ballasting, power and energy, electrical-power distribution, propulsion, navigation and positioning, obstacle avoidance, masts, manoeuvre control, communications, locator and emergency equipment, payloads. See National Defense Research Institute, *A Survey of Missions for Unmanned Undersea Vehicles (RAND)* (2009), page 46 ff.

[3]United Nations Convention on the Law of the Sea of 10 December (UNCLOS) (1982), *UNTS*, vol. 1833, page 397.

[4]U.S. Navy/U.S. Marine Corps/U.S. Coast Guard, The Commander's Handbook on the Law of Naval Operations (*NWP 1-14M*), paras. 2.3.4–2.3.6 (Edition July 2007).

they do enjoy sovereign immunity. Hence, they may only be interfered with by other States in very exceptional circumstances (e.g., in an international armed conflict). Accordingly, "USVs and UUVs engaged exclusively in Government, non-commercial service are sovereign immune craft."[5]

4. It is important to note that an independent legal status of sovereign immunity applies to UMS operating independently from another platform. Therefore, "USV/UUV status is not dependent on the status of its launch platform."[6] If the UMS is tethered to a controlling platform, it is difficult to attach to it an independent legal status.
5. This Rule is without prejudice to the belligerent right of sinking warships and other lawful targets in armed conflict.

Rule 48
In peacetime, UMS enjoy all navigational rights in accordance with the international law of the sea, *i.e.* innocent passage in territorial sea areas, transit passage in international straits, archipelagic sea lanes passage and freedom of navigation in the high seas and in the Exclusive Economic Zone (EEZ).

Commentary

1. USVs and UUVs retain the same independent rights of navigation as manned surface vessels and submarines. States in general have not (as yet) made statements to that effect, although they make use of UMS for governmental, scientific and commercial purposes. Hence, it is safe to conclude that UMS enjoy the right of freedom of navigation in the high seas and in the EEZ as well as the rights of innocent passage, transit passage and archipelagic sea lanes passage.

Rule 49
With respect to an armed conflict, States bear responsibility for internationally wrongful operations using UMS that are attributable to them. Such responsibility encompasses actions by all persons belonging to the armed forces.

Commentary

1. For an interpretation of this Rule, see the commentaries on Rules 5, 21 and 43.

Rule 50
All those involved in the conduct of operations, including attacks, using UMS, are responsible for their respective roles and, commensurate with

[5] *NWP 1-14M*, see fn. 4, para. 2.3.6.
[6] *Ibid.*

their involvement, have obligations to ensure that such operations are conducted in accordance with the applicable principles and rules of LOAC.

Commentary

1. See Commentaries on Rules 5, 22 and 44.

Rule 51

A person who wrests control of a UMS or its weapons, assumes responsibility for its subsequent use in accordance with the degree and duration of the control exercised.

Commentary

1. See the Commentaries on Rules 6 and 45.

Rule 52

During an armed conflict, UMS may be employed for attacks and for the exercise of other belligerent rights if they:

(a) are operated by the armed forces of a State;

Commentary

1. Although it is unsettled whether UMS qualify as, or are assimilated to, warships, State practice seems to suggest that they are, and will be, used not only for attack purposes but also for the exercise of other belligerent rights, such as inspection of vessels.

(b) bear the military markings of that State; and

Commentary

1. Since the exercise of belligerent rights will predominantly occur in high seas areas, there is a need for transparency because not only enemy vessels may be affected but also neutral vessels. Therefore, in times of international armed conflict, UMS should be identifiable as belonging to the armed forces of a Belligerent State.

(c) are controlled or deployed by persons subject to regular armed forces discipline.

Commentary

1. Those controlling or deploying UMS should be under regular armed forces discipline in order to ensure compliance with LOAC. The fact that the software on the UMS has been programmed by civilians is irrelevant with respect to the legal status of the UMS.

2. Control and deployment of UMS can include either direct control or the setting of mission conditions, objectives or parameters.

Rule 53
The employment of UMS for the purposes of attack is subject to the applicable principles and rules of LOAC, in particular, distinction, proportionality and the obligation to take all feasible precautions.

Commentary

1. Whereas many UMS are used for ISR or oceanography, some are designed for combat purposes, such as those employed for ASW, MCM or mine-laying. If and to the extent UMS are employed for the purposes of attack, they qualify as means of warfare,[7] and their employment is subject to weapons law and targeting law.

Rule 54
(a) UMS may be made the object of attack if they qualify as lawful targets.
(b) Enemy military UMS under Rule 52 are:

i. military objectives by nature; and
ii. subject to the concept of booty of war.

Commentary

1. Subparagraph (a) applies also to neutral UMS if they qualify as military objectives. See Rule 55.
2. This Rule reflects the customary definition of military objectives.[8] Like enemy warships, military UMS make an effective contribution to the enemy's military action by nature. Therefore, their destruction, capture or neutralization will regularly offer a definite military advantage. Non-military UMS of enemy character qualify as military objectives only if they make an effective contribution to the enemy's military action by use, purpose or location and their total or partial destruction or neutralization, in the circumstances ruling at the time, offers a definite military advantage.
3. If captured, enemy warships and military UMS constitute "booty of war" and, therefore, title to them passes without the need for prize proceedings.

Rule 55
Neutral UMS may not be attacked or captured, unless they qualify as lawful targets.

---

[7] As defined in *AMW Manual*, see chapter "Section I: Outer Space", fn. 1, Rule 1 (t).
[8] *San Remo Manual*, see chapter "Section I: Outer Space", fn. 29, para 40. See also Rule 77.

Commentary

1) As in the case of neutral merchant vessels, neutral civilian UMS are liable to attack if they make an effective contribution to the enemy's military action by use, purpose or location and their total or partial destruction, capture or neutralization, in the circumstances ruling at the time, offers a definite military advantage.[9]
2) It needs to be emphasized that capture under this Rule must be distinguished from capture as prize. The latter is not limited to vessels or UMS qualifying as lawful targets.
3) Therefore, neutral civilian UMS may become military objectives if they:

   a. Engage in belligerent acts on behalf of the enemy;
   b. Are incorporated into or assist the enemy's intelligence system;
   c. Act as auxiliaries to the enemy's armed forces; or
   d. Otherwise make an effective contribution to the enemy's military action.

4) It needs to be stressed that, at present, the capture of neutral civilian UMS seems likely to occur only in very exceptional situations. It seems unlikely that UMS would be used for the transport of cargo that could constitute contraband. Nevertheless, it may be imprudent to predict with confidence how technologies will be employed in the future.
5) Should neutral civilian UMS carry cargo qualifying as contraband, they are liable to capture.[10] The contraband cargo will be liable to condemnation in prize proceedings. If the contraband, reckoned either by value, weight, volume, or freight, forms more than one-half of the cargo, the UMS itself may be condemned by a prize court.[11]

Rule 56
Enemy UMS are not liable to capture, if they are used exclusively for non-military scientific purposes.

Commentary

1. Like enemy merchant vessels, UMS are liable to capture outside neutral waters.[12] According to Article 4 of the 1907 Hague Convention (XI)[13] and customary

[9] *San Remo Manual, ibid,* para 67.

[10] Declaration concerning the Laws of Naval War (London Declaration) (1909), *The Laws of Armed Conflict*, page 845, Article 37; *San Remo Manual*, see chapter "Section I: Outer Space", fn. 29, para 146(a).

[11] 1909 London Declaration, see fn. 10, Article 40.

[12] *San Remo Manual,* see chapter "Section I: Outer Space", fn. 29, paras 112 ff.

[13] Convention (XI) Relative to Certain Restrictions with Regard to the Exercise of the Right of Capture in Naval War, (1907), *The Laws of Armed Conflicts*, page 819.

international law,[14] "vessels charged with scientific missions are [...] exempt from capture".

2. However, they are exempt from capture only if they:

   a. Are innocently employed in their normal role;
   b. Do not commit acts harmful to the enemy; and
   c. Do not intentionally hamper the movement of enemy naval forces.

Rule 57

In so far as the use of neutral waters and ports is concerned, belligerent UMS are subject to the same rules as manned belligerent warships. Accordingly:

(a) Hostile actions by belligerent UMS are prohibited.

Commentary

1. The prohibition of hostile actions in neutral waters has been acknowledged in Article 2 of the 1907 Hague Convention (XIII)[15] and is customary in nature.[16] Accordingly, it also applies to belligerent UMS.
2. Neutral waters consist of the internal waters, territorial sea, and, where applicable, the archipelagic waters, of Neutral States.[17]
3. Hostile actions include, *inter alia*:

   a. Attack of objects and persons located in, on or over neutral waters or territory; or
   b. Laying of mines.

(b) Belligerent UMS may not use neutral waters as a base of operations or as a sanctuary.

Commentary

1. This prohibition is based on Article 5 of the 1907 Hague Convention (XIII) and customary international law.[18]

(c) Subject to the 24-hour rule, belligerent UMS have the right of stay in neutral ports or of innocent passage in neutral waters, unless the neutral coastal State has, on a non-discriminatory basis, conditioned, restricted or prohibited such stay or passage.

---

[14] *San Remo Manual*, see chapter "Section I: Outer Space", fn. 29, para. 136 (e).

[15] 1907 Hague Convention (XIII) on Neutrality in Naval War, see chapter "Section I: Outer Space", fn. 23.

[16] *San Remo Manual*, see chapter "Section I: Outer Space", fn. 29, para 15.

[17] *San Remo Manual*, *ibid*, para 14.

[18] *San Remo Manual*, *ibid*, paras 16 (b) and 17.

Commentary

1. In times of armed conflict, UMS continue to enjoy navigational rights, including innocent passage, transit passage, and, where applicable, archipelagic sea lanes passage, in neutral waters. However, a belligerent UMS may not extend the duration of its passage through neutral waters for longer than 24 hours unless this is unavoidable on account of damage or the stress of weather.[19] The 24 hours' limitation does not apply to transit passage or to archipelagic sea lanes passage.
2. A Neutral State may, on a non-discriminatory basis, condition, restrict, or prohibit the entrance to or passage through its territorial sea by Belligerent State vessels, including UMS operated for non-commercial Government purposes.[20]

Rule 58

A Neutral State may not suspend or otherwise hamper the rights of belligerent UMS as regards transit passage in international straits and passage through archipelagic sea lanes.

Commentary

1. The concepts of transit passage and of archipelagic sea lanes passage have been recognized in Articles 38 and 53 of UNCLOS.
2. In view of the importance of these passage rights, they have matured into customary international law, which applies in times of peace as well as of international armed conflict.[21]

Rule 59

(a) In the Exclusive Economic Zone or on the continental shelf of Neutral States, UMS must be employed with due regard for the rights and duties of the coastal State.

Commentary

1. In an international armed conflict, Belligerent States are not barred from the exercise of belligerent rights in the EEZ or on the continental shelf of Neutral States. However, Neutral States continue to enjoy functionally limited sovereign rights. Accordingly, when conducting hostile actions within the EEZ or on the continental shelf of Neutral States, belligerents shall, in addition to observing the basic principles and rules of the law of naval warfare, have due regard for the rights and duties of the coastal State, *inter alia*, for the exploration and exploita-

---

[19] *San Remo Manual, ibid,* para 21.

[20] *San Remo Manual, ibid,* para 19.

[21] *San Remo Manual, ibid,* para 29.

tion of the economic resources of the EEZ and the continental shelf and the protection and preservation of the marine environment.[22]

(b) Hostile actions on the high seas involving the use of UMS must be conducted with due regard for the high seas freedoms of Neutral States and for the exploration and exploitation of the "Area" under the 1982 Law of the Sea Convention.

Commentary

1. Although Belligerent States may exercise belligerent rights in the high seas, the vessels of Neutral States continue to enjoy high seas freedoms. Moreover, the seabed and subfloor beyond the limits of national jurisdiction—the "Area"[23]—enjoys a special legal status that cannot be ignored. Accordingly, Belligerent States are obliged to pay due regard to those lawful uses of the high seas and of the "Area".

(c) The obligation of due regard is without prejudice to recognized force protection measures, such as warning zones or defence bubbles.

Commentary

1. Under customary international law, defence bubbles and warning zones as well as the control of the immediate vicinity of naval and aerial operations are recognized measures of force protection that apply in times of peace and of international armed conflict.[24] They are lawful provided that they do not unduly impede the exercise of the freedoms of the high seas by neutral vessels, and that any uses of force to protect activities from interference are necessary and proportionate.
2. Belligerent States continue to enjoy the right to take all necessary measures of force protection. However, efforts should be made to ensure that the implementation of any warning zone or a defence bubble does not conflict with the requirements of a safety zone established by the neutral coastal State around artificial islands, installations or structures.

Rule 60
In sea areas beyond the territorial sea of any State, UMS operated by Neutral States for exclusively non-commercial governmental purposes must be respected.

---

[22] *San Remo Manual, ibid*, para 34.

[23] UNCLOS, see fn. 3, Article 1(1).

[24] *San Remo Manual*, see chapter "Section I: Outer Space", fn. 29, para 108; *AMW Manual*, see chapter "Section I: Outer Space", fn. 1, Rule 106.

Commentary

1. UMS operated by Neutral States for exclusively non-commercial governmental purposes enjoy sovereign immunity. They may neither be attacked, nor captured, visited, searched or otherwise interfered with.
2. This Rule applies in sea areas beyond the territorial sea of Neutral States. Of course, within neutral waters, UMS still enjoy sovereign immunity consistent with international law, and Belligerent States are obliged to refrain from any exercise of belligerent rights.

Section V: Undersea Infrastructure, Systems and Devices

Rule 61
With due regard for the rights of other States, coastal States are entitled to install, operate and maintain undersea systems and devices, whether military or civilian in nature, in their territorial sea, continental shelf and EEZ.

Commentary

1. This Rule reflects customary international law which has long recognized the rights of coastal States to install, operate and maintain underwater systems. Such systems are used for a wide variety of civilian and scientific purposes, such as maintenance and operation of offshore installations, submarine pipelines and cables, preservation of the marine environment and protection against natural disasters (*e.g.,* tsunamis).
2. They also serve a wide variety of military or security purposes. Sensors and other devices have for a long time been used for the detection of submarines and for the protection of certain parts of the coastline against potential enemies, criminals or terrorists.
3. There are only few provisions in UNCLOS (e.g., Article 258 on scientific research installations) or in other treaties addressing the installation of undersea systems and devices used for purposes other than the exploration and exploitation of the natural resources of the EEZ or the continental shelf. Of course, within their internal waters, territorial sea or, where applicable, archipelagic waters coastal/archipelagic States are entitled to install and operate such systems, whether civilian or military in nature. Coastal and archipelagic States may also install and operate undersea systems and devices, such as undersea systems and devices for the purpose of marine scientific research or in the exercise of other rights and duties in relation to the EEZ or continental shelf. Coastal States are entitled to maintain, repair and protect them.

Y. Dinstein, A. W. Dahl, *Oslo Manual on Select Topics of the Law of Armed Conflict*,
https://doi.org/10.1007/978-3-030-39169-0_5

Rule 62
Subject to the coastal States' rights (including its rights to exercise jurisdiction and its rights regarding marine scientific research) and with due regard to the rights of other States, all States are entitled to install, operate and maintain undersea systems and devices for data collection and survey activities, whether military or civilian in nature, on the continental shelf or in the EEZ of other States.

Commentary

1. Generally, States other than the coastal State may install and operate such systems in the EEZ of other States. Coastal State jurisdiction with respect to the establishment and use of structures and installations is generally limited to structures and its installations for economic purposes and to those structures and installations that may interfere with the rights of the coastal State in its EEZ.[1] Otherwise, beyond the territorial sea of any State, the freedom to construct installations permitted under international law applies (subject to part 6 of UNCLOS concerning the continental shelf[2]). Accordingly, as a rule, the coastal State does not have jurisdiction with respect to installation and structures for military or other non-economic purposes if they do not risk interfering with the coastal State's exercise of its EEZ. Coastal States do, however, have the exclusive right to authorize and regulate drilling on their continental shelves for all purposes.[3] Insofar as they are used for marine scientific research (MSR), the consent of the coastal State may be required consistent with Part XIII of UNCLOS.
2. UNCLOS does not define the term "marine scientific research", and States have not agreed on the need for—or formulation of—a particular definition. One proposed definition based in part on Article 243 of UNCLOS is that MSR refers to "those activities undertaken in ocean space to expand scientific knowledge of the marine environment and its processes."[4]
3. A systematic interpretation of the different UNCLOS provisions leads to the conclusion that MSR must be distinguished from "survey activities".[5] Accordingly, MSR does not include hydrographic surveys,[6] including military surveys, or operational oceanography.

---

[1]UNCLOS, see chapter "Section IV: Unmanned Maritime Systems", fn. 3, Article 60.

[2]UNCLOS, Article 87.

[3]UNCLOS, Article 81.

[4]G. Walker (ed.), *Definitions for the Law of the Sea*, (Leiden/Boston) (2012), page 241.

[5]See UNCLOS, see chapter "Section IV: Unmanned Maritime Systems", fn. 3, Articles 19 (2)(j), 21 (1)(g) and 40.

[6]For the importance of hydrographic surveys and nautical charting, including electronic charting, see UNGA resolution A/RES/66/231 of 24 December 2011.

4. Military surveys in foreign EEZs have been conducted by numerous States, including Russia, Japan, Australia, South Africa, China and NATO States. They cannot be considered MSR and they are not covered by the jurisdiction enjoyed by the coastal State in accordance with Article 56 (1)(b)(ii) of UNCLOS. Rather, any form of marine data collection that is not covered by the term "MSR" is a right granted either under "other internationally lawful uses of the sea"[7] or under "other pertinent rules of international law".[8] This rights may not be impeded or interfered with by the coastal State. Hence, it is safe to conclude that survey activities and operational oceanography not qualifying as marine scientific research are lawful.
5. The States having installed and operating such systems or devices in the EEZ, or whose nationals have installed and operate them, are entitled to take appropriate measures to maintain, repair and protect them. The above conclusion also applies to the continental shelf, if drilling on the shelf is not involved.

Rule 63
All States are entitled to install and operate undersea systems and devices in the high seas with due regard to the rights of other States.

Commentary

1. On the high seas, the right to install and operate such systems and devices is recognized by both the "freedom to construct artificial islands and installations" and by "other rules of international law", as provided for in Article 87(1) of UNCLOS.
2. This right is not limited to civilian or scientific systems and devices. The peaceful uses clause in Article 88 of UNCLOS, which according to Article 58(2) of UNCLOS also applies in the EEZ, does not prohibit military uses of the seas that do not qualify as a use or threat of force.
3. It must be borne in mind that in the high seas there is no prohibition of MSR. On the contrary, the freedom of the high seas includes the freedom of scientific research subject to Parts VI and XIII of UNCLOS. It must be noted that scientific research is broader than the UNCLOS term of art "marine scientific research".

Rule 64
During an armed conflict:

(a) Enemy undersea systems and devices may not be attacked, unless they qualify as lawful targets.

---

[7]UNCLOS, Article 58 (1).
[8]UNCLOS, Article 58 (2).

Commentary

1. The law of naval warfare is silent on the legal status of undersea systems and devices. It is, however, beyond doubt that they are liable to destruction or capture if they directly contribute to the enemy's military action by nature, location, purpose or use and their total or partial destruction or neutralization, in the circumstances ruling at the time, offers a definite military advantage. Hence, military systems will qualify as lawful military objectives.[9]
2. The same holds true for civilian enemy and neutral systems and devices that directly contribute to the enemy's military action.

(b) Subject to Rule 65, enemy undersea systems and devices may be captured outside neutral waters.

Commentary

1. The law of naval warfare provides no rules as to the admissibility of the capture of enemy civilian undersea systems and devices. There is, however, no cogent reason to treat such systems and devices differently from enemy vessels—whether merchant or otherwise—or enemy cargoes, which may be captured outside neutral waters.[10]
2. If an enemy undersea system or device that qualifies as a lawful target is located in neutral waters, the Neutral State is under an obligation to terminate that violation of its neutrality. If the Neutral State fails to do so, the opposing belligerent may be entitled to respond to the violation of neutrality, including, if necessary, by the use of force.[11]

Rule 65

If innocently employed in their normal role, the following enemy civilian undersea systems and devices should be exempt from capture:

(a) Undersea systems and devices exclusively used for non-military scientific missions;

Commentary

1. In principle, civilian enemy undersea systems and devices are liable to capture. Some undersea systems and devices, however, serve important scientific or humanitarian functions. Therefore, the same principles as those underlying the 1907 Hague Convention (XI)[12] should be applied. Accordingly, undersea sys-

[9]The definition of military objectives is included in Rule 77.

[10]*San Remo Manual*, see chapter "Section I: Outer Space", fn. 29, para 135.

[11]*Ibid*, para 22.

[12]1907 Convention (XI) Relative to Certain Restrictions with Regard to the Exercise of the Right of Capture in Naval War, see chapter "Section IV: Unmanned Maritime Systems", fn. 29.

tems and devices used for non-military scientific missions should be excluded from the right of capture.[13]
2. The term "should" is used in this context because there is not yet sufficient State practice that has crystallized into a rule of customary international law.

(b) Undersea systems and devices exclusively used for preventing or responding to pollution incidents in the marine environment; and

Commentary
1. Systems exclusively employed for the prevention of pollution incidents,[14] such as those monitoring and repairing submarines pipelines, should not be liable to capture.

(c) Undersea systems and devices exclusively used for the collection of data necessary to warn the civilian population of natural disasters, such as tsunamis.

Commentary
1. Systems exclusively employed for the advance warning of natural disasters (e.g. tsunamis) should not be liable to capture.
2. Of course, that protection is dependent on their innocent employment. Accordingly, such systems will no longer be protected from capture and destruction if they are used for the transmission of military data.

Rule 66
Neutral undersea systems and devices that qualify as lawful targets are liable to capture.

Commentary
1. Neutral undersea systems and devices qualify as lawful targets if they make an effective contribution to the enemy's military action, by location, purpose or use and their total or partial destruction or neutralization, in the circumstances ruling at the time, offers a definite military advantage.
2. Otherwise, neutral undersea systems and devices are protected by their neutral status, and it is prohibited for Belligerent States to capture them.
3. As distinct from neutral vessels and civil aircraft,[15] undersea systems and devices cannot at present be used for purposes—such as carriage of contraband—that would make them liable to capture under the law of prize.

---

[13]See also *San Remo Manual*, fn. 31, para 136(e).
[14]*San Remo Manual*, *ibid*, para 136(g).
[15]*San Remo Manual*, paras 67 and 146.

Section VI: Submarine Cables and Pipelines

Rule 67
States, having laid submarine cables or pipelines, or whose nationals have laid and operate such cables and pipelines, are entitled to take protective measures with a view to preventing or terminating any harmful interference.

Commentary

1. The right of all States to lay submarine cables and pipelines in high sea areas and in the EEZ, and in the continental shelf of other States has been recognized by the international law of the sea.
2. The international law of the sea regulates the relations between coastal States and the States laying submarine cables and pipelines in a general manner, by distinguishing between the different sea areas.[1] Articles 113 and 114 of UNCLOS deal with the breaking or injuring of a submarine cable or pipeline, and Article 115 provides for indemnity for loss incurred in avoiding injury to a submarine cable or pipeline.
3. However, UNCLOS is silent on certain aspects regarding submarine pipelines and cables and the question of whether and to what extent such cables and pipelines are subject to the jurisdiction of the States that own them or whose nationals have laid and operate them.
4. Article 113 of UNCLOS does not make it clear which other States also have jurisdiction over the breaking or injuring of submarine cables and pipelines beyond the territorial sea. It is, however, questionable whether only a flag State may exercise jurisdiction against foreigners regarding the breaking of cables or pipelines outside its own maritime zones.

[1]See the following provisions in UNCLOS, see fn. 58: Article 51(2)—archipelagic waters; Article 58(1)—EEZ; Article 79—continental shelf; Articles. 87(1) lit. (c), 112—high seas.

Y. Dinstein, A. W. Dahl, *Oslo Manual on Select Topics of the Law of Armed Conflict*,
https://doi.org/10.1007/978-3-030-39169-0_6

5. Article 113 of UNCLOS merely deals with the *obligation* to penalise the breaking or injuring of submarine cables or pipelines by the flag State or the State of nationality of the perpetrator. This does not imply the exclusion of an exercise of jurisdiction in other than criminal matters. States have accepted the obligation to enact domestic criminal legislation because they agree that submarine cables and pipelines must be protected. Recognition of that obligation may not be considered a waiver of exercising jurisdiction in other matters or of taking the measures necessary to protect submarine cables and pipelines against malicious interference.
6. Hence, States having laid submarine cables and pipelines, or whose nationals have laid and/or operate them, may exercise their jurisdiction in accordance with well-established principles of international law, *e.g.*, under the passive nationality and protective principle.

Rule 68

During an armed conflict, submarine pipelines and high voltage cables exclusively serving one or more Belligerent States may—if it is militarily necessary—be seized or destroyed subject to the applicable principles and rules of LOAC, in particular distinction, proportionality and the obligation to take feasible precautions.

Commentary

1. The supply of a Belligerent State with oil, gas and electricity may be crucial for war-fighting. Therefore, a Belligerent State may have a legitimate interest in denying the enemy such supply.
2. The traditional law of naval warfare is silent on submarine pipelines. Submarine telegraph cables are only addressed insofar as they are connecting occupied territory with neutral territory.
3. According to the Explanations in the San Remo Manual, "cables and pipelines exclusively serving one or more of the belligerents might be legitimate military objectives."[2] Submarine cables and pipelines are not explicitly protected against seizure or destruction if they are connecting enemy territory, which is not occupied, with neutral territory.
4. *A fortiori*, this holds true for submarine cables exclusively serving one or more Belligerent States. Such cables and pipelines do not enjoy special protection from seizure or destruction. In the past, submarine cables were liable to seizure and destruction only when imperatively demanded by the necessity of the war. However, in view of the development of the law of naval warfare, this is lawful only if they qualify as lawful military objectives and if the basic principles and rules of the law of naval warfare are observed.

[2] *San Remo Manual*, see chapter "Section I: Outer Space", fn. 29—Explanations, page 111.

Rule 69

Submarine communications cables, whether or not connecting occupied territory with neutral territory, may not be seized or destroyed even if they are serving one or more Belligerent States. Belligerent States must take care to avoid damage to such cables, unless they qualify as lawful targets.

Commentary

1. This Rule is based on the San Remo Manual paragraph 37, see fn. 31.
2. The San Remo Manual provides that "[b]elligerents shall take care to avoid damage to cables and pipelines laid on the sea-bed which do not exclusively serve the belligerents."
3. Article 54 of the 1907 Hague Regulations and the provisions of the San Remo Manual seem to reflect correctly the *lex lata* insofar as submarine pipelines and submarine high voltage cables are concerned. If they qualify as lawful military objectives, they may be seized or destroyed, provided the principle of proportionality and the obligation to take feasible precautions are observed.
4. It is, however, doubtful whether the 1907 Hague Regulations and the San Remo provisions also apply to submarine communications cables. Other than telegraphic cables, modern submarine communications cables are the backbone of global data traffic. Although they may physically connect the territories of two States, it will only in rare circumstances be possible to determine that they are "exclusively serving one or more belligerents" or one or more Neutral States. Today's submarine communications cables are interconnected. Hence, data packages will travel over routes that are unpredictable. Accordingly, it is important to distinguish between submarine communications cables and other submarine cables.

Rule 70

Submarine pipelines and high voltage cables connecting occupied territory with neutral territory must not be seized or destroyed except in the case of absolute necessity. They must likewise be restored and compensation paid when peace is concluded.

Commentary

1. This Rule reflects customary international law insofar as submarine pipelines and high voltage cables are concerned. Article 54 of the 1907 Hague Regulations provides that submarine telegraph cables "shall not be seized or destroyed except in the case of absolute necessity" and that "they must likewise be restored and compensation fixed when peace is made."
2. The same logic applies to high voltage cables. This Rule does not apply to modern submarine communications cables dealt with in Rule 67.

Section VII: Civilians Directly Participating in Hostilities

Rule 71
Civilians directly participating in hostilities lose their protection from attack for such time as they do so.

Commentary

1. This Rule is based on Article 51(3) of AP/I.[1] Non-contracting parties to AP/I support the customary principle on which that Article is based.[2]
2. The rule on direct participation in hostilities has been addressed in the ICRC Interpretive Guidance on the Notion of Direct Participation in Hostilities under International Humanitarian Law.[3] The content of the Interpretive Guidance has been contested by many commentators.
3. The loss of civilian immunity from attack due to direct participation in hostilities is limited to "such time" as the participation lasts. However, the precise duration of the timeframe involved is a matter of some controversy (particularly in "revolving door" situations).
4. When a person is a member of an organized armed group, he/she is targetable at all times.
5. The Group of Experts agreed that civilians are subject to attack when they take a direct and continuous part in armed conflict, and they cannot invoke protection from attack during temporary lulls in this participation.[4] Accordingly, the

---

[1]See chapter "Section I: Outer Space", fn. 13.

[2]*US DoD Law of War Manual*, see chapter "Section II: Cyber Operations", fn. 4 Section 5.9.1.2.

[3]International Committee of the Red Cross, *ICRC Interpretive Guidance on the Notion of Direct Participation in Hostilities under International Humanitarian Law* (2009).

[4]*US DoD Law of War Manual,* see chapter "Section II: Cyber Operations", fn. 4, at 5.8.4 (discussing the duration for which a civilian in DPH is subject to attack),; HCJ 769/02 Public Committee Against Torture v. Government of Israel para. 27, 38–40 [2006] (Isr.).

Y. Dinstein, A. W. Dahl, *Oslo Manual on Select Topics of the Law of Armed Conflict*,
https://doi.org/10.1007/978-3-030-39169-0_7

timeframe for the loss of protection due to DPH would be analogous to that of their military counterparts, as the assigned function of operating RPAs or UMSs would be considered sufficient evidence of a continuous/ongoing pattern of DPH subjecting the civilian to deliberate attack.
6. The operating of RPAs or UMSs by civilians may result in loss of protection, but this will depend on the activity in which they are engaged.
7. In view of the severe consequences of DPH the decision on whether an activity qualifies as DPH should be based on reasonably reliable information.

Rule 72
Private military contractors (PMC) retain their civilian protection as long as they are not incorporated in the armed forces—including militia or volunteer corps—and do not directly participate in hostilities.

Commentary
1. This Rule is based on Article 51(3) of AP/I. Non-contracting parties to AP/I support the customary principle on which that Article is based.[5]
2. Private military contractors may be individually hired or, alternatively, may be employees of private military corporations.
3. The status of PMC is examined in detail in the Montreux document of 2008, which points out pertinent legal obligations and good practices applicable to States using PMCs in military operations.[6] Although the Montreux document is not legally binding, it reflects the policy views of participating States.
4. Provided the following activities do not constitute direct participation in hostilities, they may be undertaken by PMCs without losing their civilian protection:

    a. Guarding of store houses;
    b. Escorting civilian dignitaries;
    c. Undertaking construction works;
    d. Engaging in food services;
    e. Engineering;
    f. Providing technical support;
    g. Carrying out instruction tasks; and
    h. Other non-combat activities.

Rule 73
If persons who are authorized to accompany the armed forces without actually being members thereof—such as supply contractors—fall into the

[5] *US DoD Law of War Manual*, Section 5.9.1.2.

[6] See *The Montreux Document On pertinent international legal obligations and good practices for States related to operations of private military and security companies during armed conflict* (2008).

power of the enemy during an international armed conflict, they are entitled to the status of prisoners of war in accordance with the third Geneva Convention of 1949 Article 4(A)(4).

Commentary

1. This Rule, which is based on GC/III, is today declaratory of customary international law applicable in international armed conflict.[7]
2. In accordance with GC/III, persons authorized to accompany the armed forces may also include:

   a. Civilian members of military aircraft crews;
   b. War correspondents;
   c. Members of labour units or of services responsible for the welfare of the armed forces;

3. The armed forces that the persons concerned are authorized to accompany must provide them with an identity card, as indicated in GC/III. Loss of an identity card does not deprive the person concerned of POW status.
4. There were divergent views within the Group of Experts about the status of persons who accompany the armed forces but participate directly in hostilities. One view was that by participating directly in hostilities, they retain POW status but may be criminally liable under domestic law for any act of hostility. By contrast, the other view was that they may lose their entitlement to POW status in certain situations in as much as they are assimilated to unlawful/unprivileged combatants. Another view, also reflected in the U.S DoD Law of War Manual, is that they are entitled to POW status, and generally cannot be held criminally liable for authorized support activities, including such support activities constituting direct participation in hostilities.
5. In any event, an enemy person who is captured shall initially be treated as a POW until his/her status has been determined. If the person claims POW rights e.g., by producing an identity card indicating that he or she is a person authorized to accompany the armed forces, but circumstances indicate that the person's status is dubious, the case should be heard according to GC/III Article 5(2).
6. Article 5 of GC/III (second paragraph) provides that "[s]hould any doubt arise as to whether persons, having committed a belligerent act and having fallen into the hands of the enemy, belong to any of the categories enumerated in Article 4, such persons shall enjoy the protection of the present Convention until such time as their status has been determined by a competent tribunal".
7. States bound by AP/I are obligated to observe Article 45(1), whereby "[a] person who takes part in hostilities and falls into the power of an adverse Party shall be presumed to be a prisoner of war, and therefore shall be protected by the Third Convention, if he claims the status of prisoner of war, or if he appears to be entitled to such status, or if the Party on which he depends claims such status on

[7] GC/III, see chapter "Section I: Outer Space", fn. 19, Article 4 A (4).

his behalf by notification to the detaining Power or to the Protecting Power. Should any doubt arise as to whether any such person is entitled to the status of prisoner of war, he shall continue to have such status and, therefore, to be protected by the Third Convention and this Protocol until such time as his status has been determined by a competent tribunal".

8. This Rule is of course limited to International Armed Conflicts. It is not applicable to Non-International Armed Conflicts.

Rule 74
Persons who are authorized to accompany the armed forces without actually being members thereof, but participate directly in hostilities, are subject to attack by the enemy.

Commentary

1. The consensus view of the Group of Experts was that LOAC does not prohibit DPH by civilians, but only exposes them to certain consequences as a result of DPH. Accordingly, DPH itself cannot be properly characterized as a breach of LOAC or as a war crime. Nonetheless, DPH may result in a violation of applicable domestic criminal laws, either as a result of the DPH itself (e.g., in U.S. law the crime of providing material support to terrorism), or as a result of its consequences (e.g., an attempted or completed violation of domestic criminal prohibitions against murder, arson, aggravated assault, etc.).

Section VIII: Civilians Participating in Unmanned Operations

Rule 75

In the context of armed conflict—whether international or non-international—civilians who conduct attacks using unmanned systems, including RPA and UMS, are directly participating in hostilities.

Commentary

1. For a general comment on the notion of DPH in LOAC, see paragraph 1 of the Commentary to Rule 12 and chapter "Section VII: Civilians Directly Participating in Hostilities".
2. Attacks fall within the range of activities that unquestionably qualify as DPH.[1]
3. Although there may be legitimate debate over the point at which support for RPA operations (see Rule 44)—such as launch and recovery, maintenance and repair, input of data into control and target acquisition systems—amount to DPH, there is general agreement among the Group of Experts that actually controlling the aircraft during certain missions and/or executing lethal attacks constitutes DPH.
4. This Rule applies to any civilian, regardless of whether he/she has been authorized to accompany the armed forces. With regard to status upon capture, see Commentary to Rule 74.
5. The notion of DPH applies during all armed conflicts, whether international or non-international in character.

[1]Sandoz, Swinarski and Zimmermann (eds.), *Commentary on the Additional Protocols of 8 June 1977 to the Geneva Conventions of 12 August 1949 (AP/I Commentary),* (Geneva: Martinus Nijhoff Publishers) (1987), at page 619: "Thus direct" participation means acts of war which by their nature or purpose are likely to cause actual harm to the personnel and equipment of the enemy armed forces. It is only during such participation that a civilian loses his immunity and becomes a legitimate target."

Y. Dinstein, A. W. Dahl, *Oslo Manual on Select Topics of the Law of Armed Conflict*,
https://doi.org/10.1007/978-3-030-39169-0_8

6. This Rule applies to civilians supporting State armed forces, to civilians associated with other State agencies or organizations (such as intelligence services), and to civilians supporting non-State organized armed groups.

Rule 76
To facilitate the implementation of the principle of distinction in an international armed conflict, States should refrain from authorizing civilians to engage in attacks using unmanned systems.

Commentary

1. LOAC does not prohibit the use of civilians to engage in activities that qualify as DPH. However, LOAC does render civilians liable to be attacked for such time as they take a direct part in hostilities. To facilitate implementation of the principle of distinction, the Group of Experts recommended that States refrain from use of civilians engaging in activities that qualify as DPH.
2. Distinction between combatants (and/or members of armed groups) and all other individuals is facilitated when combatants effectively distinguish themselves from the civilian population. Such "passive distinction" measures facilitate the ability to make lawful versus unlawful attack decisions.
3. LOAC does not recognize any category of "quasi" combatant. When civilians are known by the enemy to be engaging in DPH, the protection afforded to other civilians not so engaging may be jeopardized. This may happen because innocent civilians may erroneously be assessed as engaging in DPH and thus may be subjected to attack. Accordingly, the Group of Experts recommended that States endeavour to limit civilian roles to those functions that do not qualify as DPH, such as operating RPAs in hostilities.
4. LOAC does not indicate or restrict the manner by which individuals may be incorporated into the armed forces. Instead, this is left exclusively in the hands of domestic authorities.
5. This chapter relates exclusively to the issue of protection from enemy attack. The separate issue of capture by the enemy of civilians who are engaging in DPH has little or no relevance to RPA operators who are usually placed at some distance from the theatre of operations.

Section IX: Military Objectives by Nature

Rule 77
"Military objectives", as far as objects are concerned, are those objects which by their nature, location, purpose or use, make an effective contribution to military action and whose total or partial destruction, capture or neutralization, in the circumstances ruling at the time, offers a definite military advantage.

Commentary
1. The definition is based on Article 52 (2) of AP/I.
2. Four critical terms in the definition are "nature", "location", "purpose" and "use". This Section applies mainly to military objectives by "nature". The extent of application of the category of military objectives by "nature" is not universally agreed upon. In particular, there is disagreement on whether military objectives by "nature" constitute an absolute or relative category. Rules 78 through 84 reflect the consensus reached by the Group of Experts.
3. The definition of military objectives is confined to objects. Human beings are not military objectives for the purpose of this particular definition, but may be lawful targets as combatants or civilians directly participating in hostilities.
4. Animals can be military objectives. An example could be a mule carrying military supplies. However, animals must not be made the object of attack unless required by military necessity, *i.e.*, they constitute military objectives.

Rule 78
(a) An object can simultaneously fall within more than one of the "nature", "location", "purpose" and "use" classifications.
(b) In particular, the distinction between "nature" and "use" is that if an object qualifies as a military objective by nature it remains so classified irrespective of its current use. A military objective by "nature" can be

Y. Dinstein, A. W. Dahl, *Oslo Manual on Select Topics of the Law of Armed Conflict*,
https://doi.org/10.1007/978-3-030-39169-0_9

attacked independently of its present "use", while a military objective by "use" can be attacked only if it is actually used for military purposes.

Commentary

1. The four key terms "nature", "location", "purpose" and "use" convey different meanings, but are nevertheless interlinked. Any one classification, or combination thereof, can serve as the basis for satisfying the test of whether an object is a military objective.
2. Generally speaking, a military objective by nature can be attacked at all times. However, there are obvious exceptions. For example, an obsolete tank, aircraft, or warship—presented for display in a museum or elsewhere—would be exempted from attack. See also Rule 79.
3. Every civilian object can become a military objective by use, cf. Article 52(2) of AP/I.
4. An example is that of an art museum which—owing to its status as cultural property—does not constitute a military objective by nature. Nevertheless it can become a military objective by use if the enemy establishes, e.g., a command post there.
5. In the past broadcasting and TV stations were regarded as military objectives by nature. This view is today largely outmoded. In the past, such facilities were in most countries under centralized control and instrumental in passing information from the Government to the general public, including mobilisation orders. Today, broadcasting or equivalent functions take place from a multitude of studios and via the Internet and cell-phone networks in addition to traditional means. Broadcasting and TV stations will, however, in many situations be military objectives by use.[1]
6. As for military objectives by use in Outer Space, see Rule 10.
7. With regard to military objectives in cyberspace, see Rule 26.

Rule 79

The classification of an object as a military objective by "nature" is not altered only because it is in disuse or under repair, unless its fundamental character has changed.

Commentary

1. Even when not in use, such objects always constitute lawful targets during armed conflict. For example, an abandoned tank is still a military objective by nature, if it is capable of making an effective contribution to military action (e.g., it can be repaired/re-manned and used consistent with its nature). See also comment 2 to Rule 78.

---

[1]Note *e.g.* ICTY, *Final Report to the Prosecutor by the Committee Established to Review the NATO Bombing Campaign Against the Federal Republic of Yugoslavia*, paras. 71–79 (13 June 2000).

2. However, some objects cease to be military objectives by nature, for example, when an object that was once military equipment is turned into a museum piece, its nature has changed and it may no longer be a military objective. In this regard, see chapter "Section XV: Cultural Property" on cultural property.
3. The principles of proportionality and of precautions in attack will apply notwithstanding the classification of an object as a military objective by nature. It should be recalled that (see Rule 78a) the fact that an object is a military objective by nature does not exclude the possibility that it can also be classified as a military objective by location, purpose or use.

Rule 80

(a) An object qualifying as a military objective by "nature" can be either movable or immovable.

Commentary

1. In order to qualify as a military objective by "nature", the object in question must have an inherent characteristic or attribute that contributes effectively to military action.
2. Objects under Rule 80 are typically designed and produced in order to be used for military purposes. They can be either movable or immovable.

(b) Examples of movable military objectives by "nature" include military aircraft (other than medical aircraft); tanks and armoured personnel carriers (APCs) (other than medical transport); missiles and other weapons; military equipment; warships; UMS operated by the armed forces; military satellites; and mobile military ground stations.

Commentary

1. Rule 80 (b) is based on the AMW Manual Rule 22 (a).[2]
2. See Rules 52 and 54 on UMS.
3. See Rule 9 on military satellites.
4. The list of movable military objectives provided here is not exhaustive and is limited to the most obvious examples.
5. Military medical aircraft are entitled to certain protections from being made the object of attack. Nevertheless, medical aircraft are not civilian objects.

(c) Examples of immovable military objectives by "nature" include military fortifications, facilities and depots; military ports and airfields; missile silos; military satellite communications facilities; armaments factories; and Ministries of Defence.

---

[2]See also, DoD Law of War Manual, chapter "Section II: Cyber Operations", fn. 4, Section 6.6.1.1.

Commentary

1. Ministries of Defence are military objectives even if such Ministries are staffed in part by civilians. Of course, to the extent that a Ministry of Defence has physically separate non-defence departments, as in the case of the Swiss Federal Department of Defence, Civil Protection and Sport (DDPS), its facilities devoted exclusively to such civilian functions are not military objectives by nature.[3]
2. The list of immovable military objectives provided here is not exhaustive and is limited to the most obvious examples.

Rule 81
Military Command, Control and Communications centres (C^3) are military objectives by "nature", whether movable or immovable.

Commentary

1. The distinction between movable and immovable military objectives by "nature" does not apply to military C^3 because they could be either the one or the other.
2. Needless to say, C^3 objects are of critical importance for all military operations and their attack would likely always be prioritized by the enemy.

Rule 82
Computers that are components of weapons, weapon systems or other military systems (such as military radar stations or military Outer Space systems) are military objectives by "nature".

Commentary

1. For the purposes of this Manual, a computer is considered a component of a weapon, weapon system or other military system if it is designed from the outset or programmed specifically to play an essential role in the functioning of such weapons or systems. It can be an integral part of a weapon, a platform, a weapon system, a C3 system, etc.
2. Military computers can be either movable or immovable.
3. Computers that are military objectives by "nature" are categorically recognized as such regardless of their current use. Conversely, computers that are normally dedicated to civilian purposes may become military objectives by virtue of their actual use, e.g., in support of military action.
4. Military computers can be integral parts of a cyber infrastructure or operate on a stand-alone basis.

[3]See also, DoD law of War Manual, Section 5.6.4.

5. Military computers can be attacked by cyber, kinetic or electronic means. They can be destroyed or made to malfunction in a way advantageous to the enemy.
6. When military computers that are connected to the Internet are attacked, the expected damage or destruction to systems connected to the Internet that are not military objectives must be kept in mind.

Rule 83
In addition to the items listed in Rules 80 through 82, which are military objectives by nature, objects that will presumptively qualify as military objectives by "nature" include, but are not limited to:

Commentary

1. Rule 83 is based on the concept that, whereas some objects constitute military objectives by "nature" in all circumstances (see Rule 80–82) there are other objects that may be presumed to be military objectives by nature, but that presumption may be rebutted due to the particular circumstances prevailing at the time.
2. Although the Group of Experts determined that there was a rebuttable presumption that certain objects were military objectives by nature, they recognize that several States would prefer that the Rule be expressed in terms of "very likely" instead of "presumptively".
3. Accordingly, objects which will "presumptively" qualify as military objectives by nature will in most practical circumstances be lawful targets unless the concrete circumstances prevailing at the time indicate otherwise.
4. The distinction between a more and less absolute "nature" of military objectives is also reflected in Articles 22 and 23 of the AMW Manual.
5. This position—that there are objectives that are not military objectives by nature as an absolute matter but may necessarily be presumed to be such in the absence of circumstances to defeat that presumption—was adopted by the majority of the Group of Experts. However, there was a dissenting opinion.
6. Rule 83 deals with objects that are normally also made for civilian use, but where the potential for military use is so evident that it is more likely than not that they would make an effective contribution to military action in the near future.
7. Paragraphs (a) to (g) set forth examples of the application of this Rule. It must be noted, however, that not every example is necessarily regarded by all of the participating experts in the Group as constituting military objectives by nature.

(a) Main railway lines, main roads, bridges and tunnels;

Commentary

1. Branch railway lines are military objectives by "nature" if they connect places of military significance such as military bases, depots, weapon systems and munition factories and important airfields or harbours to the main railway network.

2. Railway lines that predominantly serve suburban commuter traffic are not military objectives by "nature".
3. Main roads include highways but may also include secondary roads when such roads would clearly serve as back-up if highways are closed. However, urban streets and avenues would not presumptively qualify as military objectives by nature.
4. Bridges and tunnels are military objectives by "nature" when they are a part of main railway lines or main roads, but they can be military objectives by "nature" for other reasons as well.

(b) If of military importance, data lines, fibre-optic cables, telephone lines and telegraph lines;

Commentary

1. Electronic communications are vital for military command and control purposes. Communication lines built for civilian purposes are likely to be used by the military in lieu of or as back-up for dedicated military lines.
2. Supporting structures, such as switchboards, servers and micro-wave datalink facilities are included among the objects that are presumptively military objectives by nature.

(c) Airports and airstrips of military significance;

Commentary

1. Airports and airstrips are of military significance when they are likely to serve as dispersal fields if military air bases are threatened by attack, or for bringing in military supplies when military air bases are closed.
2. Such airports and airstrips need to have runways of a sufficient length to serve combat or transport aircraft.
3. It must be borne in mind that attacks on civilian airports and airstrips always bring into play consideration of precautions and application of the proportionality principle.[4]

(d) Harbours of military significance;

Commentary

1. Deepwater ports that are connected to main railway lines and main roads are presumed to be military objectives by "nature".
2. Harbours that are predominantly used by coastal fisheries, and marinas for yachting are not presumed to be military objectives by "nature".

---

[4] AP/I, see fn. 15, Article 51(5)(b). The principle of proportionality is recited in para 1 of the Commentary to Rule 11.

(e) Electricity production facilities serving military needs, including power transmission facilities and equipment;

Commentary

1. Electricity is necessary for operating military bases and many weapon systems. When such military needs are (as is usually the case) provided for over the general electricity grid, the electricity production facilities and their transmission infrastructure are military objectives by "nature". See Rule 84.
2. If, however, military and civilian electricity needs are served by separate production facilities and networks, only those serving military needs are military objectives.
3. In most practical circumstances, even if military bases, radar and weapons systems etc., have their separate electricity generators, the general electricity grid will serve industry, harbours, and transportation and communications systems of military importance. In such situations, collateral damage to civilian and civilian objects must be considered under the principle of proportionality.[5]
4. It should also be kept in mind that the party subject to attack has a duty to take precautions against the effects of attacks.[6] Such "passive precautions" could for instance include the installation of emergency generators at hospitals and other particularly vulnerable civilian institutions.

(f) Oil production facilities for use by the enemy or its co-belligerents, oil terminals, refineries, crude oil and refined products storage depots, and pipelines.

Commentary

1. Fuel, predominantly based on oil, is vital for military operations. Facilities for producing, importing, refining, storing and transporting oil for use by the enemy or its co-belligerents are therefore military objectives by "nature".
2. If oil is produced and transported for export, generating revenues to finance the war effort, the facilities fall in the category of war-sustaining industries. The lawfulness of attacking such industries, as well as transportation to facilitate export, is contested. See also chapter "Section XI: Destruction of Property" Rule 101.

(g) Outer space systems and assets belonging to the armed forces.

Commentary

1. See Rule 9.

---

[5] AP/I, *ibid,* Article 51(5)(b). The principle of proportionality is recited in para 1 of the Commentary to Rule 11.

[6] AP/I, *ibid,* Article 58.

Rule 84

The status of a military objective by "nature" is not altered, even if it is also used for civilian purposes.

Commentary

1. So-called dual-use objects will always constitute lawful military objectives in light of the fact that one component of the duality involves an effective contribution to the military effort.
2. Again, the principle of proportionality must be applied even when the object under attack is a military objective by nature.

Rule 85

Attacks that treat as a single object of attack a number of clearly separated and distinct lawful targets located in a city, town, village or area containing a similar concentration of civilians or civilian objects, are considered indiscriminate and are prohibited.

Commentary

1. This Rule is not restricted to military objectives by "nature".
2. Rule 85 is based on Article 51(5)(a) of AP/I which is reflective of customary international law.
3. Rule 85 is derived from the acute need to cope with the problem of "target area" bombing that arose in WWII. The text seriously limits the possibilities in which clusters of military objectives may be attacked as if they were a single lawful target. On the other hand, it does not deny the possibility that a number of lawful targets, which are not clearly separated and distinct, may be treated as a single lawful target.
4. As the experience of WWII demonstrated, recourse to "target area" bombing may cause humanitarian devastation on an unprecedented scale because of the location of lawful targets—which are not clearly separated and distinct—within an urban centre, or other residential area. However, it must be borne in mind that, under the current LOAC, all attacks are subject to the principle of proportionality and the requirement to take feasible precautions in attack. Hence, the expected collateral damage to civilians and civilian objects must not be excessive compared to the overall military advantage anticipated.[7]
5. Although it is not contested that this Rule is based on customary international law, some States that are not contracting parties to AP/I believe that is should be confined to circumstances in which there is an intention to terrorize the civilian population or in which the attack is expected to cause excessive collateral damage.

---

[7] AP/I, *ibid,* Article 51(5)(b) and Article 57. The principle of proportionality is recited in para 1 of the Commentary to Rule 11.

6. As in other instances when the attacker is facing the risk of a breach of the principle of proportionality, the availability of precision-guided munitions (PGM) may facilitate striking lawful targets in a manner that will avoid—or, in any event, minimize—the expected collateral damage to civilians or civilian objects.

Rule 86

This Section is without prejudice to Article 56 (5) of AP/I and Article 15 of AP/II for those States Parties bound thereby. Accordingly, military objectives must not be attacked if erected for the sole purpose of protecting from attack works or installations containing dangerous forces (provided that they are not used in hostilities, except for defensive actions necessary to respond to attacks against the protected works or installations).

Commentary

1. This Rule is not restricted to military objectives by 'nature'.
2. This Rule is obligatory only for States Parties that have not made reservations concerning the provision in Article 56 (5) of AP/I and for States Parties to Article 15 of AP/II. This obligation is not considered customary international law.
3. The expression "works or installations containing dangerous forces" means dams, dikes and nuclear electrical generating stations. It does not include petrochemical works.

Section X: Civil Aviation and Civilian Airliners

Rule 87

(a) During an armed conflict, whether international or non-international, States are entitled to restrict or prohibit entry into their national airspace.

Commentary

1. The Rules in the present Section apply to States and not to non-State actors in a non-international armed conflict (NIAC). That is to say, the Rules of this Section other than Rule 90 (b) do not apply to non-State organised armed groups involved in a NIAC.
2. States have complete and exclusive sovereignty over the airspace above their land and sea territory.[1] This is reflected in both treaty[2] and customary international law.[3]
3. This Rule also applies to entry by a military aircraft into the national airspace of a co-belligerent.

---

[1]"Air" or "airspace" is defined in the AMW Manual Rule (1)(a), see chapter "Section I: Outer Space", fn. 1, as "the air up to the highest altitude at which an aircraft can fly and below the lowest possible perigee of an earth satellite in orbit. Under international law, airspace is classified as either national airspace (that over the land, internal waters, archipelagic waters, and territorial seas of any State) or international airspace (that over contiguous zones, exclusive economic zones, the high seas, and territory not subject to the sovereignty of any State)."

[2]See 1944 Convention on International Civil Aviation (Chicago Convention), ICAO Doc. 7300/9, Articles 1 and 2.

[3]Military and Paramilitary Activities in and against Nicaragua (Nicaragua v. United States of America). Merits, Judgment. *I.C.J. Reports* 1986, page 14 ff., at page 128, para. 251: "The principle of respect for territorial sovereignty is also directly infringed by the unauthorized overflight of a State's territory by aircraft belonging to or under the control of the government of another State."

Y. Dinstein, A. W. Dahl, *Oslo Manual on Select Topics of the Law of Armed Conflict*,
https://doi.org/10.1007/978-3-030-39169-0_10

4. Article 3(c) of the 1944 Chicago Convention on International Civil Aviation (Chicago Convention) states: "No state aircraft of a contracting State shall fly over the territory of another State or land thereon without authorization by special agreement or otherwise, and in accordance with the terms thereof."
5. Article 89 of the Chicago Convention sets forth: "In case of war, the provisions of this Convention shall not affect the freedom of action of any of the Contracting States affected, whether as belligerents or as neutrals. The same principle shall apply in the case of any Contracting State which declares a state of national emergency and notifies the fact to the Council."[4] The State should however avoid discriminating between aircraft of its own, neutral or allied registration and ownership when limiting access to its airspace.[5]
6. As regards transit and landing rights of scheduled air services, *i.e.* services granted access to foreign airspace under international agreements other than the Chicago Convention itself, their application to armed conflicts would be regulated by the relevant agreement, rather than Article 89 of the Chicago Convention.

(b) Subparagraph (a) is without prejudice to the rights of transit passage above international straits and of archipelagic sea lanes passage.

Commentary

1. Generally speaking, neutral States bordering international straits may not suspend, hamper or otherwise impede the right of transit passage.[6]
2. Neutral warships, auxiliary vessels, and military and state aircraft may exercise the rights of passage provided by general international law through, under and over belligerent international straits and archipelagic waters. The neutral State should, as a precautionary measure, give timely notice of its exercise of the rights of passage to the belligerent State.
3. Neutral States may not suspend, hamper or otherwise impede the right of transit passage nor the right of archipelagic sea lanes passage.[7]

Rule 88
During an international armed conflict:

(a) Belligerent military aircraft are prohibited from entering neutral national airspace.

[4]Chicago Convention, Article 9 (a) and (b), see fn. 2. See also *ibid.*, Annex 2 Rules of the air, page 3-1 (Article 3-1-10). A similar right to limit the use of airspace in "areas of active hostilities or of military occupation, and in time of war along the supply routes leading to such areas" is found in the 1944 International Air Services Transit Agreement, *UNTS*, vol. 84, page 389, Article 1.

[5]Chicago Convention, see fn. 2, Article 9.

[6]UNCLOS, see chapter "Section IV: Unmanned Maritime Systems", fn. 3, Articles 38 and 44.

[7]*Ibid.* Articles. 53 and 54.

Commentary

1. This Rule is based on the customary law of neutrality as referred to in paragraph 1 of the Commentary to Rule 18. Minor intrusions into neutral airspace occur from time to time, and are usually not challenged, but they do not call into question the general applicability of the Rule.
2. This Rule is subject to the power of the UN Security Council to exclude the application of the neutrality principle by virtue of a binding provision.

(b) Subparagraph (a) is without prejudice to the rights of transit passage above international straits and of archipelagic sea lanes passage.

Commentary

1. See the Commentary to Rule 87 (b).

(c) Neutral States have a duty to prevent or terminate the violation of their national airspace by belligerent military aircraft.

Commentary

1. This Rule is based on the customary law of neutrality as reflected in the Commentary to Rule 88 (a) and in Article 8 of the 1907 Hague Convention XIII on Neutrality in Naval War.
2. The Group of Experts agreed with the statement made in Rule 168 (b) of the AMW Manual: "If the use of the neutral territory or airspace by a Belligerent Party constitutes a serious violation, the opposing Belligerent Party may, in the absence of any feasible and timely alternative, use such force as is necessary to terminate the violation of neutrality."

(d) If a belligerent military aircraft has been forced to land, the crew must be interned for the duration of the armed conflict.

Commentary

1. This Rule is based on article 11 of the 1907 Hague Convention V.

Rule 89

Civil aviation may be prevented from using the airspace covered by a no-fly zone (within belligerent national airspace) or by an exclusion zone (within international airspace).

Commentary

1. Restrictions in aviation may take the shape of no-fly zones or exclusion zones.[8] As stated in Rule 60 in the AMW Manual, "civilian airliners (whether enemy or neutral) ought to avoid entering a no-fly or an 'exclusion zone'". However, "they do not lose their protection merely because they enter such areas."[9]
2. This Rule must be seen in relation to Rule 96 of this Manual, which urges civilian airliners to avoid areas of hazardous military activity.
3. Civil aviation may be prohibited from entering such zones if and to the extent that the Security Council has rendered a decision to that effect in the exercise of its powers under Chapter VII of the Charter of the United Nations.

Rule 90

(a) For the purposes of this Section, "civilian aircraft" means any aircraft that is not used in military, customs or police services of a State.

Commentary

1. This definition is based on Article 3(b) of the 1944 Chicago Convention.
2. The reference to the "services of a State" excludes private security and other functions.

(b) Civilian aircraft may not be attacked unless they qualify as lawful targets. Any attack on such aircraft is subject to the applicable principles and rules of LOAC.

Commentary

1. For general remarks on when objects that would ordinarily be considered civilian objects become military objectives, see paragraph 3 of the Commentary to Rule 10.
2. The principle of proportionality is addressed in general in paragraph 1 of the Commentary to Rule 11.
3. Particular considerations may arise with regard to civilian aircraft, similar but not equal (in gravity) to those that arise with regard to civilian airliners, see Rule 91 (b) with Commentary.

Rule 91

(a) "Civilian airliner" means a civilian aircraft identifiable as such and engaged in carrying civilian passengers in scheduled or non-scheduled service.

---

[8] Dealt with in the *AMW Manual*, see chapter "Section I: Outer Space", fn. 1, Section P.

[9] See also the *San Remo Manual*, see chapter "Section II: Cyber Operations", fn. 29, para 72.

Commentary

1. This definition is based on the definition made in the AMW Manual Article (1) (i).

(b) Civilian airliners are civilian objects and entitled to particular care in terms of precautions.

Commentary

1. For general remarks with regard to the duty to take feasible precautions, see paragraph1 of the Commentary to Rule 14.
2. As stated in the Commentary on the AMW Manual, the precautionary measures of identifying the object as a lawful target "must be meticulously observed" by those attacking this category of aircraft[10]; *i.e.* airliners are entitled to "particular care in terms of precautions".[11] This particular care would seem to follow from the aircraft's importance to international air navigation and the risks to which "innocent [civilian] passengers" are exposed where an armed conflict takes place.[12] The vulnerability of the aircraft and the possibility of it carrying a large number of passengers—typically civilians—argues for additional protection.[13]
3. There appears to be some reluctance to acknowledge that civilian airliners (like passenger ships) are entitled to particular care insofar as precautions in attacks are concerned. However, the Group of Experts believes that—in light of general acceptance of this notion in the San Remo Manual as well as the AMW Manual—it is appropriate to recognize that civilian airliners (like passenger ships) are entitled to supplementary protection.

(c) The mere fact that a civilian airliner is carrying some enemy military personnel, equipment, or supplies together with civilian passengers does not deprive it of its entitlement to particular care in terms of precautions.

Commentary

1. When a civilian airliner, which is supposed be engaged in carrying civilian passengers, carries enemy military personnel, it becomes a military objective by

---

[10]Commentary on the *AMW Manual*, see chapter "Section I: Outer Space", fn. 1, page 156 (Commentary to Rule 58).

[11]Commentary on the *AMW Manual*, *ibid*, page 31ff. (Commentary to Rule 1(i)), 137 (introductory Commentary to Rule 40), 155 (Rule 58) and 156 (Commentary to Rule 58). *San Remo Manual*, see chapter "Section I: Outer Space", fn. 29, page 92 (Commentary to para 13(m)).

[12]Commentary on the *AMW Manual*, see chapter "Section I: Outer Space", fn. 1, page 31 (Commentary to Rule 1(i)).

[13]As mentioned as one of two conflicting views in Commentary on the *AMW Manual*, *ibid*, page 155 (Commentary to Rule 58), see chapter "Section I: Outer Space", fn. 1.

use. However, attack of a civilian airliner can only be considered in the most extreme circumstances and in compliance with the proportionality rule, bearing in mind that civilian airliners are entitled to particular care in terms of precautions.

2. In some instances, the presence of fewer yet key enemy military personnel—such as Generals or other high ranking officers in command with significant influence over on-going hostilities—may turn the airliner into a lawful target. Even then, proportionality must always be borne in mind (see Rule 90(b)).

(d) If intercepted within a no-fly or an exclusion zone, civilian airliners continue to be entitled to particular care in terms of precautions.

Commentary

1. With regard to interception, see Rule 92 with accompanying Commentary.

Rule 92

Upon reasonable grounds, civilian airliners are liable to interception and inspection at a sufficiently safe airfield, subject to the following:

Commentary

1. The phrase "sufficiently safe" is relative and must be assessed under the circumstances ruling at the time, whereas the phrase "reasonable grounds" may, e.g., refer to suspicion that a civilian airliner is carrying contraband.[14]

(a) During an international armed conflict, interception may be exercised by belligerent military aircraft anywhere outside neutral national airspace.

Commentary

1. This Rule is based on customary international law as also expressed in the AMW Manual Rule 137.

(b) During a non-international armed conflict, interception may be exercised only by the State Party to the armed conflict and exclusively within its national airspace. If, in extraordinary situations, the respective aircraft is present in international airspace, such interception should be exercised only in the vicinity of that State's national airspace.

[14]The due regard to safety norm is also expressed in the guidelines by ICAO: International Civil Aviation Organization, Manual concerning Interception of Civil Aircraft (2nd ed. 1990), ICAO Doc. 9433-AN/926.

Commentary

1. The limitation on interception laid down in this Rule is based on general international law which makes no allowance in non-international armed conflict for the exercise of belligerent rights against aircraft of foreign nationality, and on the concern for the safety of civil aviation in international airspace.
2. An extraordinary situation might be when there is reason to believe that a hijacked airliner will be used as a suicide bomber. Any action against such aircraft would be based on the right to self-defence.
3. The term "vicinity" should be interpreted in light of the prevailing circumstances.

Rule 93
Refusal to obey an order to land or to change course may render a civilian airliner a lawful target.

Commentary

1. Civilian airliners are obliged to comply with an order issued by a State party to a conflict to land or to change course. According to customary international law, non-compliance with such orders may render a civilian airliner a military objective.
2. This is based on the San Remo Manual paragraphs 63 and 70 and the AMW Manual Rule 27(d) and 63(e).

Rule 94
The responsibility of States that provide air-traffic services for the safety of civil aviation remains intact during an armed conflict.

Commentary

1. The obligation to provide air navigation facilities for the purpose of international air navigation is found in Article 28 of the Chicago Convention. During an armed conflict, the States involved in the conflict, as well as Neutral States, will typically continue to provide such air traffic services in relation to their flight information regions (FIR).[15] The State providing air traffic services will in its flight information region "have a special responsibility for the safety of civil aircraft".[16]
2. The State responsible for providing air traffic services, should, based on the information that is available, "identify the geographical area of the conflict, assess the hazards or potential hazards to international civil aircraft operations, and

---

[15]A FIR is defined in the *AMW Manual* as "an aviation term used to describe airspace with specific dimensions, in which a flight information service and an alerting service are provided. Oceanic airspace is divided into Oceanic Information Regions and delegated to controlling authorities bordering that region. The division of authorities is done by international agreement through ICAO." See here Commentary on the *AMW Manual*, see chapter "Section I: Outer Space", fn. 1, page 239. See also Chicago Convention, fn. 2, Annex 2 Rules of the air, page 1–4.

[16]See 1990 Manual Concerning Safety Measures Relating to Military Activities Potentially Hazardous to Civil Aircraft Operations, ICAO Doc. 9554, page 14, para. 10.2.

determine whether such operations in or through the area of conflict should be avoided or may be continued under specified conditions. An international Notice to Airmen (NOTAM) containing the necessary information, advice and safety measures to be taken should then be issued and subsequently updated in the light of developments."[17]

3. A special problem occurs where such air traffic services are provided by an authority or entity located in a third State, as it might be difficult to gather sufficient information on the relevant risk levels in the foreign areas where it provides the said services. For instance, the Swiss company Skyguide—Swiss Air Navigation Services Limited—provides air traffic services for Switzerland, but also for adjoining areas in Germany, Austria, France and Italy.[18] Should a non-international or international armed conflict take place in any of these areas beyond the Swiss borders, the authorities of the relevant territories may restrict or close their airspace although the airspace is normally handled by Skyguide. No such authority to close or restrict national airspace would seem to have been delegated to the company by the abovementioned States, but it is to be expected that the company will issue statements regarding the perceived threat level. Here, its potential responsibility for damage or destruction following insufficient warnings to civilian air traffic may presumably be reduced considering that it has less access to situational information on the current or planned military operations than would be the case for a national agency providing such services.

Rule 95

(a) During an armed conflict, States should—whenever necessary for the safety of civil aviation—restrict access to their national airspace (in whole or in part) by civilian airliners.

Commentary

1. See Rule 87 (a) with Commentary for general remarks on States' entitlement to restrict their national airspace. The present Rule is non-binding in character and concerned with situations when States should use their entitlement in this regard.
2. The failure of States to restrict access to their national airspace may contribute to tragic events such as the downing of Malaysia Airlines flight MH17 above Hrabove, Ukraine, on 17 July 2014.

[17] 1990 Manual Concerning Safety Measures Relating to Military Activities Potentially Hazardous to Civil Aircraft Operations, see fn. 16, page 14, para. 10.3.

[18] See Skyguide, Annual Report 2015 (Geneva 2016) pages 22 and 28.

3. The Chicago Convention Annexes 11, 15 and 17 place a due diligence obligation upon the State to ensure the safety of its airspace.[19] Correspondingly, under Chicago Convention Annex 11, close cooperation must be established between air traffic services authorities and military authorities, and coordination of activities potentially hazardous to civil aircraft must also be established.[20]
4. Where a State has knowledge of a credible and concrete risk to airliners, and where restriction on the use or closure of its airspace is the only reasonable measure available, the State is obligated to act accordingly. Otherwise, a State is only obliged—at some indeterminate stage during the intensification of military activities in the airspace—to close parts of its airspace to foreign civil aviation. An alternative to prohibiting flights at all altitudes may be the prohibition against flying below a certain altitude.[21]
5. The Dutch Safety Board's consideration of States involved in NIACs shows that few States actually practice the closing (in whole or in part) of their airspace.[22]
6. Regardless of whether the territorial State decides to keep its airspace open, the State where the operator is registered may obligate the carrier not to use a specific foreign airspace or, at the very least, may place restrictions on the use of that airspace by its aircraft.[23]

---

[19]Chicago Convention, see fn. 2, Annex 11, Art. 2.17, Annex 15, Art. 5.1.1.1 (l) and (n), and Annex 17, Arts. 2.1.2, 2.4.3, and 3.1.3. Whether the Standards and Recommended Practices contained in annexes to the Chicago Convention are binding on the State parties is on the other hand disputed. For the ICAO view, see Res. A36-13 (2007) Consolidated statement of continuing ICAO policies and associated practices related specifically to air navigation. See as well statements by the ICAO Secretary General Raymond Benjamin in a letter to state civil authorities, 24 July 2014, page 2, para. 5.

[20]Articles 2.17 and 2.18. See also Manual Concerning Safety Measures Relating to Military Activities Potentially Hazardous to Civil Aircraft Operations, see fn. 16.

[21]A slightly different view might be held by the Dutch Safety Board. See Dutch Safety Board, Crash of Malaysia Airlines flight MH17 Hrabove, Ukraine, 17 July 2014 (The Hague, October 2015) page 172. Here, the Manual Concerning Safety Measures Relating to Military Activities Potentially Hazardous to Civil Aircraft Operations, see fn. 11, para. 3.1.1 holds that "[i]n the event that a sudden outbreak of armed hostilities or any other factors preclude this normal co-ordination process, appropriate State and ATS authorities, civil aircraft operators and pilots-in-command of aircraft must assess the situation based on the information available and plan their actions so as not to jeopardize safety."

[22]Dutch Safety Board, Crash of Malaysia Airlines flight MH17 Hrabove, Ukraine, 17 July 2014 (The Hague, October 2015) pages 199–205 (Libya, Northern Mali and, after the MH17 incident, the Ukraine).

[23]Dutch Safety Board, Crash of Malaysia Airlines flight MH17 Hrabove, Ukraine, 17 July 2014 (The Hague, October 2015) pages 173–174, 221, 232 and 242.

(b) A State must keep under review the level of danger to civil aviation under its air traffic control and inform the relevant foreign actors of any imminent dangers to aviation in the airspace for which it is responsible.

Commentary

1. The Group of Experts came to the conclusion that, as opposed to Rule 94 (a), the present Rule is binding upon States as an expression of customary international law. It appears that some States regard the general practice in this context as a matter of "best practice" rather than binding custom.
2. The Group of Experts was of the opinion that this duty is comparable to the duty of a coastal State to inform other States of a minefield in its territorial sea which poses imminent danger to shipping.[24] It is, however, difficult to find State practice and *opinio juris* supporting an obligation to inform more generally on changes in the risk level during an armed conflict,[25] although the non-binding ICAO Manual Concerning Safety Measures Relating to Military Activities Potentially Hazardous to Civil Aircraft Operations indicates that the territorial State should do this.[26]

Rule 96
Civilian airliners should avoid areas of potentially hazardous military activity, even if civil aviation has not been restricted or prohibited in the respective airspace.

---

[24]The Corfu Channel Case, Judgment 9 April 1949, *I.C.J. Reports* 1949, pages 4–169, page 22: "The obligations incumbent upon the Albanian authorities consisted in notifying, for the benefit of shipping in general, the existence of a minefield in Albanian territorial waters and in warning the approaching British warships of the imminent danger to which the minefield exposed them. Such obligations are based, not on the Hague Convention of 1907, No. VIII, which is applicable in time of war, but on certain general and well-recognized principles, namely: elementary considerations of humanity, even more exacting in peace than in war; the principle of the freedom of maritime communication; and every State's obligation not to allow knowingly its territory to be used for acts contrary to the rights of other States." More generally, a coastal State is under an obligation to "give appropriate publicity to any danger to navigation, of which it has knowledge, within its territorial sea" according to UNCLOS, see chapter "Section IV: Unmanned Maritime Systems", fn. 1, Article 24 (2).

[25]Dutch Safety Board, Crash of Malaysia Airlines flight MH17 Hrabove, Ukraine, 17 July 2014 (The Hague, October 2015) pages 207 and 262. The Dutch Safety Board report recommends on page 264 that ICAO member States "[e]nsure that States' responsibilities related to the safety of their airspace are more strictly defined in the Chicago Convention and the underlying Standards and Recommended Practices, so that it is clear in which cases the airspace should be closed."

[26]1990 Manual Concerning Safety Measures Relating to Military Activities Potentially Hazardous to Civil Aircraft Operations, see fn. 16, page 14, para. 10.3. See also Dutch Safety Board, Crash of Malaysia Airlines flight MH17 Hrabove, Ukraine, 17 July 2014 (The Hague, October 2015) pages 173 and 208–209. Chicago Convention, see fn. 2, Annex 15 Article. 5.1.1 here holds that "[a] NOTAM shall be originated and issued promptly whenever the information to be distributed is of a temporary nature and of short duration or when operationally significant permanent changes, or temporary changes of long duration are made at short notice, except for extensive text and/or graphics."

Commentary

1. This Rule is based on Rule 54 of the AMW Manual and is a corollary non-binding Rule to the one applicable to States in Rule 95, in order to ensure the safety of civil aviation in time of armed conflict.

Section XI: Destruction of Property

Rule 97
It is specifically prohibited to destroy, damage or seize enemy private or public property unless such destruction is justified by military necessity under the principles and rules of LOAC.

Commentary

1. This Rule is based on Article 23(g) of the 1907 Hague Regulations and the customary international law of armed conflict.[1] The Rule is, in principle, applicable to all domains of warfare (air, sea, land, cyber and space).
2. Military necessity includes those measures imperatively required in order to achieve the aims or ends of warfare, and (hereunder) having a reasonable connection to those ends. Military necessity must be distinguished from political, economic or diplomatic needs.
3. Destruction of property qualifying as military objectives is *a fortiori* also necessary, and lawful. The practical scope of the Rule thus relates to enemy civilian property during international armed conflict.
4. The notion of property is not defined by applicable treaties. The notion of property must therefore be understood in light of its ordinary (dictionary) meaning. All tangible, movable or immovable items as well as real property fall within the notion of "property".

[1]The rule appeared at the Brussels Conference (1874), *The Laws of Armed Conflicts*, page 21, Article 13(g). Today, its customary status is expressed for example in Henckaerts and Doswald-Beck, *International Committee of the Red Cross Customary International Humanitarian Law (CIHL),* (Cambridge: Cambridge University Press) (2005, reprint 2009), vol. I, rule 50, and the Rome Statute of the International Criminal Court (Rome Statute) (1998), *The Laws of Armed Conflicts*, page 1309, Article 8(2)(b)(xiii).

Y. Dinstein, A. W. Dahl, *Oslo Manual on Select Topics of the Law of Armed Conflict*,
https://doi.org/10.1007/978-3-030-39169-0_11

5. There is an increasing legal debate as to whether intangible objects are to be considered property. The Group of Experts did not reject the possibility that, for example, data can qualify as "property" under LOAC. On the other hand, the majority of the Group was of the opinion that intellectual property does not qualify as "property" under LOAC.
6. Necessary destruction, damage or seizure of property may be connected to an attack, but it may also result incidentally from sheer movements and manoeuvers of armed forces. By way of example, buildings, roads, bridges, fences and cultivated fields may be destroyed or damaged as a result of the weight and speed of military vehicles (such as tanks).
7. Military necessity may require and thus justify the destruction, damage or seizure of enemy property in the course of or in preparation for an attack (as defined in LOAC) or other military operations.
8. Destruction, damage or seizure of enemy property may occur in a manner that is incidental to movement and manoeuver of troops. Such destruction, damage or seizure may be considered as an unavoidable consequence of warfare and is thus justified on the basis of military necessary.
9. Military necessity must be assessed by the commander based on the facts reasonably available to him/her under the circumstances prevailing at the time.
10. The present Rule applies without prejudice to rules governing special protection from attack, such as the rules providing protection of cultural property (see chapter "Section XV: Cultural Property")[2] and medical facilities.[3]
11. The present Rule is without prejudice to the rules governing destruction, seizure and confiscation in the context of belligerent occupation.
12. In non-international armed conflict, the issue of what property is regarded as enemy property is more complex than in international armed conflicts, inasmuch as the State may seize, destroy or damage property under its jurisdiction in conformity with its domestic law.

Rule 98
In an international armed conflict, any extensive destruction or seizure of property, not justified by military necessity and carried out unlawfully and wantonly constitutes a war crime.

---

[2]AP/I, see chapter "Section I: Outer Space" I, fn. 13, Article 53, Convention for the Protection of Cultural Property in the Event of Armed Conflict (1954), *The Laws of Armed Conflicts,* page 747, Article 4. Second Protocol to the Hague Convention of 1954 for the Protection of Cultural Property in the Event of Armed Conflict (1999), *The Laws of Armed Conflicts*, page 1037, Article 6. See also Rule 98 and chapter "Section XIV: Humanitarian Assistance" of this Manual.

[3]AP/I, *ibid,* Article 12, and GC/I, see chapter "Section I: Outer Space", fn. 19, Article 19. *AMW Manual,* see chapter "Section I: Outer Space", fn. 1, Section L. *San Remo Manual*, see chapter "Section I: Outer Space", fn. 29, para 169–183.

Commentary

1. The present Rule is based on the language of Article 147 of GC/IV, which of course uses the language of "grave breach" of the Geneva Convention now understood to mean war crime (cf. Article 8 of the Rome Statute of the International Criminal Court).
2. The Rule is, in principle, applicable to all domains of warfare (air, sea, land, cyber and outer space).[4]
3. For all practical purposes, wantonness is the opposite of necessity (see Rule 97).[5] Wanton destruction is particularly egregious destruction of property that is not motivated by lawful aims of warfare, but is random conduct or conduct motivated by a desire to inflict destruction as an end in itself.[6] In order to qualify as a war crime the destruction or seizure of property must also be unlawful and extensive. An example of such wanton destruction is the burning of Kuwaiti oil wells by the retreating Iraqi forces in 1991 that was carried out without military necessity.
4. Destruction of property qualifying as a military objective is never considered wanton. Destruction of enemy property justified by military necessity in accordance with Rule 97 is never wanton.
5. The prohibition applies regardless of whether the property is State owned or owned by private persons or legal entities.
6. Destruction of property is generally accompanied by the counterpart term, damage (see Rule 97). The term damage does not appear in the present Rule because it is not mentioned in the text of Article 147 of GC/IV.
7. The term seizure is used in this Rule as a corollary of Rule 97. It encapsulates the notion of appropriation of property mentioned in Article 147 of GC/IV.
8. The present Rule is without prejudice to the rules governing destruction, seizure and confiscation in the context of belligerent occupation.

Rule 99

(a) It is prohibited to attack, destroy, remove or render useless objects indispensable to the survival of the civilian population for the specific purpose of denying them for their sustenance value to the civilian population or to the adverse Party, whatever the motive, whether in order to starve out civilians, to cause them to move away, or for any other motive.

Commentary

1. This Rule is based on Articles 54(2) of AP/I and 14 of AP/II.

---

[4]See Rule 97 with regard to the scope of application.

[5]As already expressed in the Lieber Code.

[6]*In re* List and Others (Hostages Trial), *United States Military Tribunal at Nuremberg*, in Annual Digest and Reports of Public International Law Cases (1948), at page 647.

2. Under AP/I, exceptions exist for this Rule, such as for objects used by an adverse party "as sustenance solely for the members its armed forces" or "if not sustenance, then in direct support of military action". However, actions against this latter category of objects forfeiting protection may not be taken if they "may be expected to leave the civilian population with such inadequate food or water as to cause its starvation or force its movement".
3. Customary international law prohibits the starvation of civilians as a method of warfare.

(b) In recognition of the vital requirements of any Party to the conflict in the defence of its national territory against invasion, derogation from the prohibition in subparagraph (a) may be made by a Party to the conflict within such territory under its own control where required by imperative military necessity.

Commentary

1. This Rule is based on Article 54(5) of AP/I.
2. The Rule applies to the defence of a Belligerent State's own territory against an invading enemy force. That is to say the tactics of "scorched earth" cannot be used by the invading enemy, nor can such tactics be used by a State not taking action in the defence of its own territory.

Rule 100
Rules 97 and 98 are without prejudice to specific rules on capture as booty of war or as prize.

Commentary

1. Capture of property as booty of war or for prize is governed by specific rules.[7] When capture or destruction is lawful according to these specific rules, the acts are also *ipso facto* required by military necessity and will not amount to acts of wantonness.

Rule 101
In a non-international armed conflict, destruction or seizure is not prohibited when directed against items illegally appropriated or produced (such as oil or opium) by non-State armed groups and used by them to generate revenue for the purpose of continuing the hostilities.

---

[7] Capture of war booty is a recognized lawful practice in customary international law, see CIHL, Rule 49, see fn. 1. Capture for prize at sea is dealt with in the San Remo Manual, see chapter "Section I: Outer Space", fn. 29, para 135–158, and in the *AMW Manual*, see chapter "Section I: Outer Space", fn. 1, Section U.

Commentary

1. The Group of Experts was aware of the fact that this Rule is not accepted by all States. However, the majority of the Group believed that there is sufficient practice of States (as manifested in Syria since 2015) to substantiate the text.
2. Nevertheless, the majority of the Group of Experts could not agree on the conceptual underpinning for this new Rule. Different views were put forward with the view to providing a proper rationale.
3. One view, based on a wider—largely US—perception of LOAC, is that lawful targets of attack (and *a fortiori* property that it is lawful to destroy or seize, see paragraph 3 of the Commentary to Rule 97) include not only "war-fighting" or "war-supporting" but also "war-sustaining" enemy objects that qualify as military objectives.[8]
4. Another view, is that there is a *sui generis* rule relating to action against fleets of oil-tanker trucks (irrespective of their destination).
5. A third view is that this is a land alternative to naval or aerial blockade. Ordinarily, exports can be barred only through the imposition of a blockade. Yet, blockade as a method of warfare is irrelevant to (i) land-locked enemy countries in an international armed conflict, or (ii) any insurgent-held areas in a non-international armed conflict (since the construct of neutrality is alien to non-international armed conflicts). Absent the possibility of blockade, it has been argued that enemy exports can be barred through attacks against truck convoys.
6. Finally, there was a minority of the Group of Experts that acknowledged that the conduct described in this Rule would not qualify as a war crime, but that took the view that it would still be in violation of the law of non-international armed conflict.
7. In any event, destruction and seizure of items that are illegally (according to domestic law) appropriated or produced by non-State actors, is lawful according to the domestic law of most States.

[8] See *US DoD Manual*, see chapter "Section II: Cyber Operations", fn. 4, at page 237–238.

Section XII: Surrender

Rule 102
Enemy military personnel and civilians who have been directly participating in hostilities who manifest the intent to surrender and who comply with the additional requirements of Rules 103 and 104 are *hors de combat* and may not be denied quarter.

Commentary

1. "Manifest" means to express or demonstrate clearly.
2. The Rule applies to combatants and civilians participating directly in hostilities. The norm may also apply to other persons who are eligible for POW status.[1] On persons eligible for POW status, see Rule 105.
3. Enemy personnel may offer to surrender themselves (and the military equipment under their control) to a Belligerent State. The obligation to accept valid offers to surrender is a LOAC rule that does not preclude a Belligerent State from prohibiting surrender by its own personnel within its own national jurisdiction. Domestic law, however, does not alter the LOAC obligation to accept such surrender, and the fact that a surrender was offered in violation of domestic law does not invalidate the surrender under international law.
4. The prohibition against denying quarter to those manifesting the intent to surrender is based on Article 23 (d) of the 1907 Hague Regulations[2] and on

[1] GC/III, see chapter "Section I: Outer Space", fn. 19, Article 4.

[2] 1907 Hague Regulations, see chapter "Section I: Outer Space", fn. 13, Article 23: "In addition to the prohibitions provided by special Conventions, it is especially forbidden: . . . (d) to declare that no quarter will be given."

Y. Dinstein, A. W. Dahl, *Oslo Manual on Select Topics of the Law of Armed Conflict*,
https://doi.org/10.1007/978-3-030-39169-0_12

Article 40 of AP/I.[3] To deny quarter to an enemy means to refuse to accept an offer to surrender.

5. The requirement to accept surrender applies whether or not the person surrendering is able to fight.
6. Persons who resist in any way or otherwise continue to pose a threat to the enemy cannot be regarded as having surrendered.
7. It is unlawful to kill or injure persons who have surrendered regardless of whether or not they have combatant status.
8. If an individual soldier manifests the intent to surrender while his/her comrades continue to fight, difficult situations may arise. The following considerations should be borne in mind:

   a. During an engagement, it may be impossible to distinguish between the individual who has attempted to offer his or her surrender and his/her comrades who continue the fight; and
   b. The soldier purporting to surrender may be conspiring with his/her comrades, acting perfidiously in order to lure the enemy into a trap. See Rule 104 and the important conditions set out in Rule 103.

9. In a non-international armed conflict, any persons—including members of armed forces and of non-state armed groups—may give themselves up for capture and thereby receive the protection specified in Rule 106.

Rule 103
In order to be valid, surrender must meet the following conditions:

(a) The offer to surrender is communicated in a clear manner to the enemy.

Commentary

1. This Rule is based on Article 41(2) of AP/I and Article 23(c) of the 1907 Hague Regulations, which has customary law status.
2. If the forces of a Belligerent State are unaware of the intent to surrender, they cannot be expected to desist from further attacks.
3. If a person makes an attempt to communicate an intent to surrender in a manner that is not clear, the condition is not met. However, if circumstances permit, the enemy should make reasonable efforts to seek clarification.
4. Surrender must be distinguished from retreat. The mere fact that retreating personnel have disposed of their weapons, ought not to be confused with the concept of *laying down of arms* referred to in Common Article 3 of GC I-IV, which manifests an intent to surrender.
5. In land warfare, traditional ways of communicating intent to surrender are to lay down one's weapons and to raise one's arms. The display of a white flag,[4]

---

[3] AP/I, see chapter "Section I: Outer Space", fn. 13, Article 40: "It is prohibited to order that there shall be no survivors, to threaten an adversary therewith or to conduct hostilities on this basis."

[4] 1907 Hague Regulations, see chapter "Section I: Outer Space", fn. 13, Article 32.

which once meant only a request to parley, is today also used as a means of communicating an intention to surrender.

6. In naval warfare, the traditional signal of surrender is to strike the flag.
7. Unlike land warfare, the practice of air warfare does not reveal any commonly accepted indication of an aircrew's wish to surrender.[5]
8. Rule 103 (a) applies *mutatis mutandis* to capture in non-international armed conflict (see paragraph 9 of the Commentary to Rule 102).
9. It must be borne in mind that in an international armed conflict waged between two or more adverse parties that do not share a common language, linguistic problems may arise in the communication of an intent to surrender. Every effort must be made to surmount such difficulties.

(b) The offer to surrender is genuine.

Commentary

1. For further discussion, see Commentary to Rule 104.
2. In air warfare, aircrews or aircraft operators—as with persons in land or naval warfare—must assess in good faith whether persons are offering a genuine surrender based on the information that is available to them at the time. There is no obligation to presume that a person is *hors de combat* if there is doubt as to the genuineness of a surrender.
3. The obligation to manifest the intention to surrender lies with the individual who offers to surrender. Thus, the offer to surrender must be communicated under circumstances where it can be properly received and understood by the enemy forces.
4. Whether an offer to surrender must be regarded as genuine relies on a balancing of several factors, including:

   a. Time available for deliberation and for consideration of ambiguous offers of surrender.
   b. Risk to the attacking party.
   c. Cultural mores of the enemy forces with respect to surrender.
   d. Prior history with respect to the conduct of the enemy forces in similar situations.
   e. Enemy history of compliance with LOAC, including with respect to perfidy.
   f. Other considerations that may bear on the genuineness of the offer.

5. If there is indeed a genuine offer to surrender and other requirements set out in the present Section are met, the surrendering person is protected from attack for as long as he or she remains in the power of the capturing party. For comments on the duty to release captured enemy combatants, see Rule 105(a).

---

[5] *AMW Manual*, see chapter "Section I: Outer Space", fn. 1, Comment 2 on Rule 128.

6. A previous reneging on an offer to surrender or the resumption of hostile acts subsequent to an offer to surrender can constitute *prima facie* evidence that the offer is not genuine.
7. Rule 103(b) applies *mutatis mutandis* to capture in non-international armed conflict.

(c) The offer to surrender must be unconditional

Commentary
1. This requirement is reflected in Article 23(c) of the 1907 Hague Regulations, which provides the surrender must be "at discretion".
2. The expression, "at discretion" implies that if the person offering to surrender poses certain conditions, and these conditions are accepted, then (and only then) the surrendering individual becomes *hors de combat.*[6]

(d) Those offering to surrender have laid down their arms and do not engage in any further hostile acts.

Commentary
1. This Rule is based on Article 41(2) of AP/I.
2. A person engaging in hostile acts cannot be regarded as having laid down his/her arms.
3. Hostile acts may include acts like transmitting intelligence to the enemy. Such acts are not compatible with surrender.
4. Killing or injuring an adversary while feigning surrender amounts to the war crime of perfidy.[7] For States Parties to AP/I the same applies to capturing an enemy while feigning surrender.
5. Rule 103 (c) applies *mutatis mutandis* to capture in non-international armed conflict (see paragraph 9 of the Commentary to Rule 102).

(e) No attempt is made to evade capture.

Commentary
1. This Rule is based on Article 41(2) of AP/I.
2. A person who tries to evade capture has not laid down his/her arms in the legal sense, and is not *hors de combat*. He/she can therefore be attacked.
3. An individual on the ground or at sea who surrenders to an aircraft must stay visible to the aircraft and obey any instructions given until he/she can be taken into custody by any aircraft, vessel or ground forces called to the scene by the capturing aircraft. For situations where capture is under no circumstances feasible, see Rule 104.

---

[6] DoD Law of War Manual, see chapter "Section II: Cyber Operations", fn. 4, 5.9.2.3.

[7] AP/I, see chapter "Section I: Outer Space", fn. 13, Article 37.

4. Rule 103 (d) applies *mutatis mutandis* to capture in non-international armed conflict (see paragraph 9 of the Commentary to Rule 102).

(f) Those who offer to surrender strictly comply with instructions from the adversary.

Commentary

1. See paragraph 3 of the Commentary to Rule 103(e).
2. The obligation to comply strictly with instructions issued by the adversary also applies to ground forces wishing to surrender to an aircraft. See further the Commentary to Rule 104.
3. Rule 103 (e) applies *mutatis mutandis* to capture in non-international armed conflict (see paragraph 9 of the Commentary to Rule 102).

Rule 104

An offer to surrender may not be genuine if manifested in circumstances in which it is not feasible for the opposing party to accept the surrender. Accordingly, the offer of surrender by ground forces to an aircraft may be invalid if taking the forces into custody is not feasible in the prevailing circumstances.

Commentary

1. This issue was subject to lengthy discussions among the Group of Experts.
2. Two scenarios may illustrate the problem:
   a. A military aircraft flying over enemy positions behind enemy lines discovers an enemy tank and observes that its crew has raised their hands. There are two issues here: (i) whether the conditions laid down in Article 103(a) through (e) appear to have been fulfilled and (ii) whether capture can be effected under Rule 104.
   b. For example, if a small unit the size of a patrol operating in contested territory encounters an enemy infantry battalion offering to surrender, capture may not be possible. This example must, however, be understood without prejudice to Article 41(3) of AP/I and the duty to release combatants who have fallen into the power of the enemy under unusual circumstances that prevent their evacuation.[8] See also Rule 105(a).
3. Surrender by ground forces to aircraft raises problems of factual impracticability in the taking of such persons into custody. Different views were expressed

[8]AP/I, see chapter "Section I: Outer Space", fn. 13, Article 41(3): "When persons entitled to protection as prisoners of war have fallen into the power of an adverse Party under unusual conditions of combat which prevent their evacuation as provided for in Part III, Section 1, of the Third Convention, they shall be released and all feasible precautions shall be taken to ensure their safety." The customary status of this rule is confirmed by several military manuals, including the *US DoD Manual,* see chapter "Section II: Cyber Operations", fn. 4, para 9.9.3.

among the Group of Experts. According to some of the Experts, the possibility of the taking of such persons into custody is irrelevant to the genuineness of the offer to surrender. Another view would preclude ground forces from gaining *hors de combat* status vis-a-vis an aircraft because an offer to surrender cannot be genuine when it is factually impossible for the opposing party to accept. According to an intermediate view, the validity of the offer by forces surrendering to an aircraft has to be determined on a case-by- case basis (e.g., when there is an effective possibility of capture owing to the proximity to the contact zone).

4. The conditions laid down in Rule 103(a)-(e) require mutually understood communication between those surrendering and the capturing personnel. See, in particular, paragraph 3 of the Commentary to Rule 103(b).
5. The crews of military aircraft are duty bound to accept genuine offers of surrender, but an offer is genuine only if made in circumstances in which it is feasible for the adversary to accept it. In practice, much depends upon the time available for deliberation and the level of risk to the attacking party.

Rule 105

(a) Unless released, captured persons who are entitled to Prisoner of War status must be transported, as soon as it is practicable, to a Prisoner of War Camp.

Commentary

1. This Rule is based on Articles 19 ff of GC/III which expresses customary LOAC.
2. Captured enemy personnel must be evacuated as soon as possible to camps situated far enough from the combat zone to be “out of danger”. The notion of “out of danger” must be understood according to the circumstances. For example, the phrase has been understood to mean that the camp should be out of range of enemy artillery.
3. The duty to transport to a Prisoner of War Camp applies to all those entitled to POW status who are not released, repatriated or hospitalized prior to the time of internment. When circumstances do not permit the legally required evacuation due to “unusual conditions of combat”, those who are Party to AP/I must release enemy personnel in accordance with Article 41(3) of AP/I.[9]
4. Captured personnel who are not entitled to POW status may be interned in a camp other than a Prisoner of War Camp. However, the fundamental guarantees enumerated in Article 75 of AP/I must be observed. See also Rule 106 with regard to non-international armed conflicts.
5. POWs who are accused and convicted of crimes in accordance with applicable domestic or international law (see chapter “Section XVII: International Criminal

[9]See fn. 170.

Law") may, instead of being interned in a POW camp, serve sentences of punitive confinement under the same conditions as those applying to members of the armed forces of the Detaining Power.

(b) Captured enemy combatants may be detained temporarily in a forward transit, screening or detention facility, or a field hospital.

Commentary

1. Article 19 of GC/III allows for temporary internment in a danger zone owing to the prevailing circumstances.

Rule 106

In non-international armed conflicts, the legal status of Prisoner of War does not apply, but all captured persons must at all times be treated humanely in conformity with applicable international standards, regardless of whether the captured persons are subjected to criminal prosecution.

Commentary

1. Common Article 3 of the GC I-IV provides minimum safeguards standards for persons who have been deprived of their liberty. Those guarantees are reflective of customary LOAC. See also Article 5 of AP/II.
2. As a minimum, all persons deprived of their liberty in a NIAC must be:

   a. Treated humanely without any adverse distinction founded on race, colour, religion or faith, sex, birth or wealth, or any other similar criteria;
   b. Protected against violence to life and person, torture, or cruel, humiliating and degrading treatment; and
   c. Afforded the judicial guarantees recognized as indispensable by civilized peoples, if subject to criminal proceedings. In this regard, see chapter "Section XVII: International Criminal Law".

Section XIII: Search and Rescue

Rule 107
For the purposes of this Manual, "Shipwrecked" means persons, whether military or civilian, who are in peril at sea or in other waters during an armed conflict as a result of misfortune affecting them or the vessel, aircraft, or spacecraft carrying them.

Commentary

1. This definition draws from Article 12 of GC/II and Article 8(b) of AP/I but clarifies that spacecraft can also yield a shipwreck situation. It must be taken into account that the AP/I definition (which includes all civilians and all types of waters) is not binding on non-contracting Parties. Moreover, there is not yet enough State practice related to the status of former occupants of spacecraft.
2. Although the crews of neutral aircraft or ships are not included in the list of protected persons under Article 13 of the GC/II, the Group of Experts agreed that the term shipwrecked also applies to them. This is true, in particular, if their vessel, aircraft or spacecraft has been attacked.
3. An individual who is without vessel, aircraft, or spacecraft at sea or other waters should be presumed to be at peril unless there is contrary information indicating the individual is at sea or other waters by choice. For example, an individual who chooses to swim into the water to avoid a land-based attack is not *hors de combat* due to shipwreck. Neither are the members of a water-borne combat unit who have entered the water voluntarily.
4. "Shipwrecked" are military or civilian persons in a perilous situation at sea or on any other waters following a misfortune and who refrain from all acts of hostility. See Rule 108.
5. Under Article 8(b) of AP/I the concept is expanded to include persons, who are in peril at sea or in other waters *(e.g.* lakes). The term "shipwreck" means

Y. Dinstein, A. W. Dahl, *Oslo Manual on Select Topics of the Law of Armed Conflict*,
https://doi.org/10.1007/978-3-030-39169-0_13

shipwreck from any cause and includes forced landings at sea by or from aircraft (first paragraph of Article 12 of GC/II).

6. There is no evidence in general State practice to the effect that persons can reach a coast and nevertheless remain "shipwrecked" although such position has been taken by some.

Rule 108

Shipwrecked and other persons *hors de combat* are protected from attack, provided that they abstain from any hostile act and no attempt is made to evade capture or escape.

Commentary

1. This Rule is derived from Article 41 of AP/I. See also Article 23(c) of the 1907 Hague Regulations and Article 3 of GC/II.
2. For this context, there are two categories of persons *hors de combat*:

   a. Those who have clearly expressed an intention to surrender; and
   b. Those who are incapacitated. This latter category falls into three subsets: sick; wounded; and shipwrecked.
      Upon due consideration, the majority of the Group of Experts decided not to retain the separate category of Article 41(a) of AP/I, *i.e.* persons "in the power of an adverse Party", in view of the fact that such category is irrelevant for the purpose of the present Section.

3. Note that clearly expressing an intention to surrender indicates more than mere desire to do so. See chapter "Section XII: Surrender".
4. Although, as a term of art, the expression "*hors de combat*" is reserved for combatants, for the purposes of this Rule the concept covers incapacitation of both combatants and civilians who have directly participated in hostilities since the latter will, by definition, no longer be participating in hostilities when *hors de combat*.
5. The presumption of *hors de combat* status for an individual at sea or other waters during an armed conflict is rebutted if he or she commits a hostile act, or attempts to escape or evade capture.
6. The status of *hors de combat*, including that of "shipwrecked", applies both in international and in non-international armed conflict.
7. Although Article 41(2) of AP/I conditions *hors de combat* status on the absence of an "attempt to escape" the Group of Experts decided that in case of shipwreck the condition must be extended so that no attempt to evade capture is made.

Rule 109

(a) Persons parachuting from an aircraft in distress may not be made the object of attack during their descent unless they engage in hostile acts.

(b) Upon reaching the ground in territory controlled by the adverse party the parachutists from an aircraft in distress shall be given an opportunity

to surrender, unless it is apparent that they are engaging in a hostile act or attempting to evade capture.

(c) Airborne troops are not protected by this Rule.

Commentary

1. This provision is based on Article 42 of AP/I.
2. Although not expressly referred to by AP/I as *hors de combat*, parachutists from aircraft in distress may be assimilated to that status during their descent, unless they engage in hostile acts.
3. The assumption is that upon landing in a territory controlled by the enemy the parachutist from the aircraft in distress will surrender. The enemy must provide him/her with an opportunity to do so.

Rule 110

A person who is *hors de combat* remains as such until the circumstances that gave rise to that status are altered.

Commentary

1. Whether an individual is *hors de combat* depends on facts and is based on the circumstances ruling at the time.
2. An individual can be *hors de combat* for a particular reason, may thereafter lose that status as a result of a change in the circumstances that rendered him/her *hors de combat*, but may then become *hors de combat* for another reason. For example, a shipwrecked individual may be rescued—in which case he/she is no longer *hors de combat* by reason of shipwreck—but may also be wounded thus acquiring the status of *hors de combat* due to injury.
3. An individual who is *hors de combat* is not a lawful target, regardless of the reason why he or she is *hors de combat*.
4. It goes without saying that anyone who engages in hostile acts can no longer be protected as *hors de combat.*

Rule 111

(a) A shipwrecked combatant remains *hors de combat* during rescue provided he or she refrains from all acts of hostility.

Commentary

1. If someone is *hors de combat* due to shipwreck, he/she will be considered *hors de combat* due to shipwreck throughout a rescue.
2. This Rule is consistent with the definition of "shipwrecked" found in Rule 107.

(b) "During rescue" means the time during which a shipwrecked individual is in the process of being rescued from sea or other waters. This includes

the time during which the person is being assisted onto land, or into an aircraft, a vessel or another conveyance.

Commentary

1. This Rule is consistent with the definition of "shipwrecked" found in Rule 107 and Article 8 (b) of AP/I. It is designed to clarify that point during a rescue operation at which a shipwrecked individual might regain combatant status. See also, Rule 112 and its Commentary.

Rule 112

A combatant or other person, after being rescued and transported onto land, or into an aircraft, a vessel or another conveyance capable of transportation to a safe location, is no longer *hors de combat* by reason of being shipwrecked.

Commentary

1. The precise moment when a rescue concludes, thus terminating an individual's *hors de combat* status by reason of shipwreck, depends on the circumstances. Generally, it includes the time during which the individual is being lifted into a helicopter or a vessel designed for normal conveyance of personnel.
2. The requirement that the ultimate conveyance that triggers the termination of *hors de combat* status be "capable of transportation to a safe location" is meant to exclude life boats and other vessels designed to preserve life but not provide transportation to safety. The conveyance need not be designed specifically to carry passengers, such as a ferry, but it has to be seaworthy or otherwise capable of transport in the conditions prevailing at the time.
3. By way of example, shipwrecked individuals are *hors de combat* while being lifted into a rescuing helicopter but are no longer *hors de combat* upon reaching the helicopter. Conversely, shipwrecked individuals being lifted into an emergency life boat remain *hors de combat* until ultimately rescued from the lifeboat and moved onto a conveyance capable of carrying them to land or otherwise removing them from peril.
4. Once a rescue is complete, the individuals are no longer *hors de combat* due to shipwreck. However, they may become *hors de combat* for another reason. See Commentary to Rule 110.

Rule 113

The conduct of search and rescue operations does not cause military aircraft, vessels or other conveyances, or military personnel conducting the operations, to be protected from attack, regardless of whether the person being rescued is civilian or military.

Commentary

1. The status of military personnel and of military conveyances as lawful targets does not change due to the mere fact that they are engaged in search and rescue operations, whether for the benefit of either combatant or civilian shipwrecked.
2. Even if the persons who are the object of rescue are *hors de combat* by reason of shipwreck, their protected status does not (i) extend to the military personnel or the military conveyances searching for or rescuing them; or (ii) endure after they have been lifted to the aircraft or vessel and are no longer in water.
3. A separate issue arises with regard to persons who remain *hors de combat* due to being wounded. Regardless of whether they continue to be protected after having been lifted to an aircraft or vessel, the status of the vehicle as a lawful target remains unchanged. Whether an attack on the vehicle is consistent with LOAC is subject to proportionality and precautions in attack, if the persons rescued are civilians.

Rule 114

(a) "Combat Search and Rescue (CSAR) operations" enjoy no protection from attack.

(b) "CSAR operations" means the rescue, or attempted rescue, of combatants in distress, whether at sea, on land, or in Outer Space, when the rescue or attempted rescue occurs during an armed conflict and is carried out by combatants.

Commentary

1. If a search-and-rescue operation is conducted during armed conflict by military personnel or conveyances, for the benefit of combatants in distress, then it is a combat search-and-rescue operation (CSAR). Such an operation enjoys no protection from attack. Similarly, if the rescued persons were civilians in distress, the rescuers and the operation itself would not enjoy protection even if the shipwrecked persons being rescued would.
2. See Commentary to Rule 113 regarding the propriety of including wounded individuals in proportionality analyses.

Rule 115

(a) Medical aircraft lose their specially protected status if they engage in conduct inconsistent with the requirements of that status.

(b) Such inconsistent activities include CSAR operations.

Commentary

1. Medical aircraft, that is to say, aircraft exclusively employed for the removal of wounded and sick and for the transport of medical personnel and

equipment,[1] enjoy specially protected status within the scope of Articles 36 and 37 of GC/I, Articles 25–31 of AP/I and customary LOAC.

2. Under GC/I, the specially protected status of medical aircraft is dependent on the location of the medical aircraft and on, when so required, a prior agreement between the parties to the conflict.[2]
3. Even if there is a valid reason for discontinuing the specific protection of medical units or medical transports, a warning must be issued first.[3] The warning may take various forms. In many instances, it can simply consist of an order to cease the harmful act within a specified period. The time-limit must be reasonable in order to give an opportunity for the unlawful acts to be stopped or to allow removal to a place of safety of the wounded and sick within the medical units or medical transports, prior to any attack. In some cases, it may be reasonable to insist on immediate compliance with a warning. However, even in these cases, the principle of proportionality and the requirement to take feasible precautions in attack apply. Medical aircraft do not become lawful targets unless the warning remains unheeded.[4]
4. Paragraph 3 of this commentary is without prejudice to the exceptional circumstance of a medical aircraft engaging in attack, in which case a warning may become redundant when self-defence measures are resorted to.
5. In the absence of a specific agreement between parties to an armed conflict, medical aircraft should refrain from conducting search-and-rescue operations because it may lead to the conclusion that they are engaging in combat operations. For that reason, this Rule clarifies that if these medical aircraft engage in search-and-rescue operations they lose their protection. However, this Rule notes the requirement that any attacker give the medical aircraft a warning and a reasonable time-limit to heed that warning.

Rule 116

Hospital ships and coastal rescue craft lose their specially protected status if they engage in conduct inconsistent with the conditions of their protection and if the requirements of the law of naval warfare are met.

Commentary

1. Hospital ships, that is to say, ships built or equipped specially and solely with a view to assisting the wounded, sick and shipwrecked, to treating them and to transporting them,[5] and coastal rescue craft, *i.e.* craft employed by the State or

---

[1] GC/I, see chapter "Section I: Outer Space", fn. 19, Article 36.

[2] AP/I, see chapter "Section I: Outer Space", fn. 13, Articles 25–27. *AMW Manual,* see chapter "Section I: Outer Space", fn. 1, Rules 77 and 78.

[3] *AMW Manual, ibid,* Rule 38.

[4] GC/I, see chapter "Section I: Outer Space", fn. 19, Article 21.

[5] GC/II, *ibid,* Article 22.

by the officially recognized lifeboat institutions for coastal rescue operations,[6] enjoy special protection in accordance with Article 34 of GC/II and Article 22 of AP/I. This means that hospital ships as well as coastal rescue craft may be neither attacked nor captured.

2. Non-compliance with the conditions of their protection as laid down in Article 30 of the GC/II will usually render hospital ships and coastal rescue craft liable to capture. However, if they commit "acts harmful to the enemy" they will become liable to attack subject to the requirements set out in paragraph 3.
3. Hospital ships and coastal rescue craft committing acts harmful to the enemy may be made the object of an attack only after a due warning has been given, naming in all appropriate cases a time limit, and after such warning has remained unheeded.[7] Acts *not* amounting to acts harmful to the enemy are listed in Article 35 of GC/II. However, in so far as the use of secret codes for communications systems is concerned, see the position taken in the San Remo Manual paragraph 171 as to subsequent practice.[8] The text of GCII, which governs the use of hospital ships, does not make it clear whether such a vessel can itself indulge in rescue operations or, alternatively, it merely transports and treats those rescued by other craft.
4. It is important to note that hospital ships are entitled to additional protections under LOAC that are not accorded to coastal rescue craft. This is illustrated in Article 27 of GC/II, which states that "[u]nder the same conditions as those provided for in Articles 22 and 24 [referring to hospital ships], small craft employed by the State or by the officially recognized lifeboat institutions for coastal rescue operations, shall also be respected and protected, so far as operational requirements permit."
5. The San Remo Manual's assessment of customary international law, besides confirming in Rule 49 that hospital ships must be warned that their exemption from attack is endangered and cannot be targeted unless they do not heed the warning, specifically states that hospital ships can be targeted only "as a last resort."[9] The San Remo Manual does not articulate a requirement that coastal rescue craft be given a warning or that they be attacked only "as a last resort."[10]

Rule 117
Non-military aircraft other than medical aircraft, and non-naval vessels other than hospital ships and coastal rescue craft, which are engaged in search and rescue operations, may not be attacked unless they:

[6]GC/II, *ibid*, Article 27.
[7]GC/II, *ibid*, Article 34.
[8]See as well *US DoD Manual*, chapter "Section II: Cyber Operations", fn. 4, para 7.12.2.7.
[9]*San Remo Manual*, see chapter "Section II: Cyber Operations", fn. 4, para 51.
[10]*San Remo Manual*, *ibid*, para 52.

(a) Assist a rescued enemy combatant, or other person liable to capture, to escape or evade capture;

Commentary

1. Civilians engaged in efforts to return combatants to the battlefield are directly participating in hostilities (see chapter "Section VII: Civilians Directly Participating in Hostilities") and thus no longer protected against attack.

(b) Refuse a demand to surrender an enemy rescued combatant; or

Commentary

1. A refusal to surrender an enemy rescued combatant may also amount to direct participation in hostilities.

(c) Otherwise make an effective contribution to the enemy's military action.

Commentary

1. The Rule in (c) serves as a reminder that objects may become lawful targets by conduct not covered in (a) or (b), such as the transmission of military intelligence to the enemy.

Rule 118

The Rules of this Section are without prejudice to the right of the parties to the conflict to enter into agreements on the protection of aircraft, vessels or other vehicles employed for search and rescue.

Commentary

1. This Rule reflects the principle that parties to the conflict may always agree on the creation of additional protections that are not required by LOAC, and that search and rescue operations represent an understandable area for such additional protections.[11]

---

[11] See for example, AP/I, chapter "Section I: Outer Space", fn. 13, Article 26 (1) and 27 and 28 (4).

Section XIV: Humanitarian Assistance

Rule 119

(a) If the civilian population in occupied territory is not adequately provided with food, medical supplies, clothing, bedding, means of shelter or other supplies or care essential to its survival, the Occupying Power must undertake, facilitate, or allow relief consignments, which are humanitarian and impartial in character, and conducted without adverse distinction.

(b) If the Occupying Power does not provide the civilian population in the occupied territory with adequate humanitarian relief as provided for in (a), it must consent to humanitarian relief consignments by other States or impartial international humanitarian organizations as described in Rules 120 and 121.

Commentary

1. "Humanitarian aid" or "humanitarian relief" is not defined by treaty LOAC,[1] but GC/I-IV and AP/I provide the key elements thereof: "medical and hospital stores", "essential foodstuffs, clothing and tonics intended for children under fifteen, expectant mothers and maternity cases",[2] "other articles if the resources of the occupied territory are inadequate",[3] "clothing"[4] and "bedding, means of shelter, other supplies essential to the survival of the civilian population".[5]

---

[1]For the purposes of this Manual the expressions "humanitarian aid", "humanitarian assistance" and 'humanitarian relief' are synonymous.

[2]GC/IV, see chapter "Section I: Outer Space", fn. 19, Article 23.

[3]GC/IV, *ibid,* Article 55.

[4]GC/IV, *ibid*, Article 59.

[5]AP/ I, see chapter "Section I: Outer Space", fn. 13, Article 69 (1).

Y. Dinstein, A. W. Dahl, *Oslo Manual on Select Topics of the Law of Armed Conflict*,
https://doi.org/10.1007/978-3-030-39169-0_14

2. The obligation to take care of the needs of the civilian population is most clearly regulated with regard to occupied territories: the Occupying Power has the duty of "ensuring the food and medical supplies of the population"—to the fullest extent of the means available to it—and it is obliged to, in particular, "provide necessary foodstuffs, medical stores and other articles if the resources of the occupied territory are inadequate".[6]
3. In case the needs of the "whole or part" of the civilian population cannot be met by the Occupying Power, the latter shall agree to humanitarian relief consignments for the benefit of the said population, which may be undertaken either by States or impartial humanitarian organizations, and shall facilitate them "by all the means at its disposal".[7]
4. In a situation of occupation, the Occupying Power may verify that the relief consignments are purely humanitarian in their nature (see Commentary to Rule 125(a)), a process that may take some time, but it cannot withhold consent indefinitely.

Rule 120

(a) If the civilian population of any territory under the control of a party to the conflict, other than occupied territory, is not adequately provided with food, medical supplies, clothing, bedding, means of shelter or other supplies or care essential to its survival, relief consignments, which are humanitarian and impartial in character and conducted without adverse distinction, must be undertaken and facilitated.

(b) Where humanitarian relief consignments are offered by other States or impartial international humanitarian organizations, this can be undertaken only subject to the consent of the territorial State.

(c) Such consent cannot be withheld arbitrarily.

Commentary

1. This Rule deals with international armed conflicts in situations that do not entail belligerent occupation. As for non-international armed conflicts, see Rule 129.
2. It is primarily a responsibility for each State to take care of the humanitarian needs of the civilian population within its territory. Hence, the territorial State has the primary role in the initiation, organization, coordination, and implementation of humanitarian assistance within its territory.[8]

[6]GC/IV, see chapter "Section I: Outer Space", fn. 19, Article 55.

[7]GC/IV, *ibid*, art. 59.

[8]See UN GA Res 46/82 (1991), Annex, paragraph 4.

3. With regard to international armed conflicts, the current status of the law is that consent of the controlling State is required. This follows explicitly from Article 70(1) of AP/I.[9]
4. It is generally agreed, however, that consent cannot be withheld arbitrarily.[10]

Rule 121
Withholding of consent can be arbitrary if it is not compatible, *inter alia,* with other obligations under applicable principles and rules of LOAC, or if it is unreasonable given the needs of the civilian population in the prevailing circumstances.

Commentary

1. The phrase "applicable principles and rules of LOAC" is explained in paragraph 5 of the Commentary to Rule 2.
2. With regard to the notion of "arbitrarily", justification for the denial of an offer of humanitarian assistance is crucial. Withholding consent to external assistance is not arbitrary where:

   a. A State is capable of providing, and willing to provide, an adequate and effective humanitarian assistance on the basis of its own resources;
   b. An affected State has accepted appropriate and sufficient assistance from elsewhere; or
   c. The relevant offer is not extended in accordance with the principles of neutrality, impartiality, and non-discrimination, as laid down in Rule 127. Conversely, where an offer of assistance is made in accordance with the foregoing and no alternate sources of humanitarian assistance are available, there would be a strong inference that a decision to withhold consent is arbitrary.[11]

Rule 122
Consent is not required if the Security Council has made use of its powers under the Charter of the United Nations to authorize in a binding manner relief actions for the civilian population in any situation of armed conflict.

[9] AP/ I, see chapter "Section I: Outer Space", fn. 13, Article 70 (1); "Parties" in plural, since the consignments may travel through several countries.

[10] See the position in the *US DoD Manual*, see chapter "Section II: Cyber Operations", fn. 4, para 17.8.1: "States may withhold consent for, inter alia, legitimate military reasons, but should not arbitrarily withhold consent".

[11] Report ILC, 66th Session, No. A/69/10 (UN, New York, 2014), Chapter V.

Commentary

1. This Rule is based on the powers vested in the Security Council by Chapter VII of the Charter of the United Nations to authorize measures binding upon States.
2. Refusal to abide by a binding decision of the Security Council is, by definition, arbitrary as well as unlawful under Article 25 of the Charter of the United Nations.

Rule 123

Offers to provide humanitarian relief consignments to the civilian population of another State shall not be regarded as:

(a) Interference in the armed conflict;
(b) An unfriendly act; or
(c) An interference in the domestic affairs of the State concerned.

Commentary

1. Subparagraphs (a) and (b) are derived from AP/I 70 (1).
2. This Rule is embedded in the judgement of the ICJ in the Nicaragua Case.
3. As clarified by the court in the Nicaragua Case, this Rule is confined to the "provision of food, clothing, medicine and other humanitarian assistance, and it does not include the provision of weapons, weapons systems, ammunition, or other equipment, vehicles, or material which can be used to inflict serious bodily harm or death". This requirement reflects the prohibition against intervening in matters that are essentially internal to the State concerned. In this regard the ICJ stated that "there can be no doubt that the provision of strictly humanitarian aid to persons or forces in another country, whatever their political affiliations or objectives, cannot be regarded as unlawful intervention, or as in any other way contrary to international law".[12]

Rule 124

Humanitarian relief consignments may be provided in accordance with Rule 119 and 120 either by States or by impartial humanitarian organizations, such as the International Committee of the Red Cross.

Commentary

1. There are no formal requirements as to who may seek to provide humanitarian relief consignments subject to the conditions set out in Rule 125.
2. The International Committee of the Red Cross is the paradigmatic example of an impartial humanitarian organization, but of course it is not the only one.

[12]ICJ, Nicaragua v. United States of America, see chapter "Section X: Civil Aviation and Civilian Airliners", fn. 3, paragraphs 242 and 97.

Rule 125

(a) States should allow and facilitate rapid and unimpeded passage of humanitarian relief consignments, equipment and personnel in accordance with Rules 119 and 120, subject to technical arrangements.

Commentary

1. This Rule deals in a combined manner with occupied and non-occupied territory. However, it must be underscored that in occupied territory, the obligation borne by the Occupying Power (under Rule 119) is unqualified.[13]
2. Although the distribution of humanitarian relief consignments must not be arbitrarily impeded, it may be subjected to technical arrangements.
3. Obviously, compliance with technical arrangements may be time consuming. However, it must not become an excuse for an arbitrary withholding of consent to humanitarian relief action.

(b) Technical arrangements may derive from operational exigencies and may include matters such as:

i. Verification that the relief supplies do not contain weapons, munitions, military equipment or other supplies reasonably expected to be used for military purposes;

ii. Regulation of the relief consignment in order to prescribe times and routes in such a way as to avoid hampering military operations and to conform to the maximum extent with security requirements;

iii. Establishment of air corridors for the transit of relief air transports; or

iv. Organisation of air drops or landings.

Commentary

1. The mentioned list is illustrative and not exhaustive.

(c) Technical arrangements under sub-paragraph (b) must in no case be misused in order to make the provision of relief consignments inoperative or to delay the forwarding of relief unduly.

Rule 126

(a) Personnel of impartial humanitarian relief organizations, acting within their mandates, must be respected and protected and must not be made the object of attack or of any action that arbitrarily prevents them from discharging their mandate. The protection extends to their humanitarian transports, installations, goods and activities.

[13] See 1949 Geneva Convention Relative to the Protection of Civilian Persons in Time of War, chapter "Section I: Outer Space", fn. 19.

(b) Only in the case of imperative military necessity may the activities of personnel of impartial humanitarian relief organizations be limited or their movements temporarily restricted.

Commentary

1. Paragraph (a) of this Rule is based on Article 71(2) of AP/I and customary LOAC, as expressed in Article 8(2)(b)(iii) and Article 8(2)(e)(iii) of the Rome Statute.[14] Paragraph (b) of this Rule is based on Article 71(3) of AP/I.
2. Although AP/I provides that the protection of humanitarian relief personnel applies only to "approved", *i.e.* authorized, humanitarian personnel as such, the overwhelming majority of practice does not specify this condition.[15] The notion of authorization refers to the consent received from the party to the conflict concerned to work in areas under its control.[16] However, as Article 71(3) provides, "Each Party in receipt of relief consignments shall, to the fullest extent practicable, assist the relief personnel referred to in paragraph 1 in carrying out their relief mission. Only in case of imperative military necessity may the activities of the relief personnel be limited or their movements temporarily restricted."
3. United Nations personnel delivering humanitarian aid enjoy specific protection under the Convention on the Safety of United Nations and Associated Personnel, as their safety and security shall be ensured and they shall not be made the object of attack or of any action that prevents them from discharging their mandate.[17]
4. The word "respect" means "to spare, not to attack", while "protect" means "to come to someone's defence, to lend help and support."[18] Thus, it is prohibited to attack, to kill, to maltreat or injure humanitarian relief personnel in any way, and there is also an obligation to come to their rescue.
5. The obligation to respect and protect relief personnel applies to all the parties to the conflict, which should instruct their armed forces not to attack such personnel.

---

[14]See as well *AMW Manual*, see chapter "Section I: Outer Space", fn. 1, at page 36 ff. and UN Security Council resolutions 2175 (2014) and 2286 (2016)

[15]The *US DoD Law of War Manual*, see chapter "Section II: Cyber Operations", fn. 2, at page 1035, does not specifically require the humanitarian personnel to be approved or authorized, but notes that the safety of humanitarian personnel is a legitimate consideration for a Government in consenting to their operations.

[16]AP/I, see chapter "Section I: Outer Space", fn. 13, Article 71(1), and CIHL, see chapter "Section XI: Destruction of Property", fn. 1, Rule 31.

[17]Convention on the Safety of UN and Associated Personnel (1994), *UNTS*, vol. 2051, page 363, Article 7.

[18]*AP/Commentary*, see chapter "Section VIII: Civilians Participating in Unmanned Operations", fn. 1, to Article 10, para 446.

Rule 127
Humanitarian relief personnel, transports, installations, goods and activities may lose special protection if the relief actions are not:

Commentary

1. Non-compliance with the conditions listed in subparagraph (a) through (d) may deprive the humanitarian personnel and objects of their special protections but does not affect their civilian protection unless the personnel are directly participating in hostilities or, in the case of objects, they are effectively contributing to the enemy's military action.

(a) Exclusively humanitarian and impartial in character;

Commentary

1. See Rule 119 (a).

(b) Conducted without any adverse distinction;

Commentary

1. LOAC requires non-discrimination in its application and prohibits adverse discrimination based on sex, race, nationality, religion, political opinions or any other similar criteria.
2. The prohibition of adverse distinction does not imply that special treatment of persons with particular needs would be prohibited.[19]
3. It would not be arbitrary for a State to refuse to give consent to a provision of humanitarian assistance that would be based on the making of an adverse distinction among the recipients of that assistance.

(c) Executed in accordance with the terms of their mission; or

Commentary

1. The mission refers to the agreement concluded between the organisation or neutral State providing the relief action and the concerned State.

(d) In compliance with the technical arrangements issued by the States or parties concerned.

Commentary

1. For examples of technical arrangements, see Rule 125 (b).

---

[19] *AP/Commentary*, *ibid*, to Article 70(2), para 2825.

Rule 128
Whenever circumstances permit, parties to the conflict should suspend attacks in order to permit passage of humanitarian relief consignments.

Commentary

1. Due to an insufficiency of State practice and *opinio juris* supporting this Rule, the Group of Experts decided to avoid the use of mandatory language (such as "must" or "shall").
2. The notion of "circumstances permit" is generally understood to reflect considerations of military necessity.

Rule 129
In principle, the Rules relating to the provision of humanitarian assistance apply to both international and non-international armed conflicts *mutatis mutandis*.

Commentary

1. AP/II provides that relief actions in non-international armed conflicts should be undertaken subject to the consent of the High Contracting Party concerned. As stipulated in Article 18 (2) of AP/II, such consent is always required, i.e., even in situations where an area controlled by non-State actors borders on an adjacent State so that humanitarian access can take place without passing through areas controlled by the incumbent Government.
2. Although *de jure* there is no treaty requirement of insurgent consent, *de facto*—should the insurgents be in control of the relevant territory—their consent to the humanitarian operation will become indispensable for the provider of humanitarian assistance. Efforts must, however, also be made to secure the consent of the incumbent Government.

Section XV: Cultural Property

Rule 130
"Cultural property" means movable or immovable property, whether secular or religious and irrespective of origin or ownership, which is of great importance to the cultural heritage of every people. Examples include buildings and other monuments of historic, artistic or architectural significance; archaeological sites; artworks, antiquities, manuscripts, books, collections thereof, and collections of reproductions thereof; scientific collections; and archives. The term "cultural property" extends to buildings whose main and effective purpose is to preserve or exhibit movable cultural property and to refuges intended to shelter it, as well as to centres containing a large amount of movable or immovable cultural property.

Commentary

1. The definition of "cultural property" in this Rule is based on Article 1 of the 1954 Hague Convention for the Protection of Cultural Property in the Event of Armed Conflict.
2. The phrase "of every people" in Article 1 of the 1954 Hague Convention is capable on its face of two meanings, *i.e.* "of all peoples jointly" or "of each respective people". The practice of States Parties to the Convention varies in terms of the interpretation of the phrase, and opinions are therefore divided as to the correct approach. Whether specific property is of sufficient importance is for all relevant States, including the State on whose territory it is situated, to determine and is an assessment that must be made in good faith.
3. Where they are not "cultural property" in the technical sense, buildings such as educational institutions, libraries, archives and places of worship, along with objects such as artworks and books, are still protected by LOAC as civilian objects. That said, as is the case with any other object of a civilian nature, the

Y. Dinstein, A. W. Dahl, *Oslo Manual on Select Topics of the Law of Armed Conflict*,
https://doi.org/10.1007/978-3-030-39169-0_15

items referred to in this paragraph may become military objectives, *e.g.* by virtue of use.

4. These Rules can also apply in occupied territory, see Article 5 of the 1954 Hague Convention.

Rule 131

In an armed conflict, it is prohibited to make any use of cultural property or of its immediate surroundings for purposes likely to expose the property to destruction or damage unless this is imperatively required by military necessity.

Commentary

1. This Rule is based on Articles 4(1) and (2) as well as Article 19(1) of the 1954 Hague Convention. See also Article 16 of AP/II. The Rule is consistent with customary LOAC protections of cultural property applicable in both international and non-international armed conflicts.
2. Subject to waiver for reasons of imperative military necessity, uses of cultural property or its immediate surroundings that are prohibited by Rule 131 include, by way of example:

   a. Positioning a missile battery or anti-aircraft gun inside or alongside a historic structure, whether to take tactical advantage of the location or to shield the battery or gun from attack;
   b. Incorporating a historic structure into a defensive line; and
   c. Using a historic structure as a field headquarters or armoury.

3. The use of cultural property or that of its immediate surroundings need not expose it to attack for it to violate the Rule. Rule 131 prohibits, subject to imperative military necessity, any use of cultural property or of its immediate surroundings for purposes likely to expose the property to damage resulting in the likelihood of material harm to cultural property.
4. In all cases, any use of cultural property or of its immediate surroundings for purposes likely to expose the property to destruction or damage is not prohibited if imperatively required by military necessity.
5. A party to the conflict's use of cultural property or of its immediate surroundings for purposes likely to expose the property to destruction or damage does not automatically relieve an opposing party of its obligation not to attack the property (see Rule 132(a)). That is, use contrary to Rule 131 does not of itself make it lawful to attack cultural property. It is prohibited to attack cultural property unless it becomes a lawful object of attack (see Rules 9 and 10 with Commentaries) and unless military necessity imperatively requires waiver of the obligation to refrain from any act of hostility directed against such property (see Rule 132(a)).
6. Destruction of property that does not qualify as cultural property is dealt with in chapter "Section XI: Destruction of Property".

Rule 132

(a) It is prohibited to make cultural property the object of attack unless it is a military objective and military necessity imperatively requires waiver of the obligation to refrain from any act of hostility directed against such property.

Commentary

1. This Rule is based on Articles 4(1) and (2) of the 1954 Hague Convention. However, the concept of military objective is rooted in customary international law and it has been introduced in Article 6(a)(i) and (ii) of the Second Protocol (of 1999) to the 1954 Hague Convention. It must be noted, nevertheless, that the Second Protocol is not as widely ratified as the original Convention.

(b) Where cultural property becomes a military objective and military necessity imperatively requires waiver of the obligation to refrain from any act of hostility directed against it, any decision to attack the property should be taken only by an officer of appropriate seniority.

Commentary

1. This paragraph of Rule 132 is based on the general practice of States. When parties to the conflict are bound by the Second Protocol (of 1999) to the 1954 Hague Convention, Article 6(c) provides in mandatory terms that any decision to invoke military necessity to attack cultural property must be taken by an officer commanding a force equivalent in size to at least a battalion, unless circumstances do not permit.

(c) Where cultural property becomes a military objective and military necessity imperatively requires waiver of the obligation to refrain from any act of hostility directed against it, a party to the conflict should give advance warning whenever circumstances permit.

Commentary

1. Where parties to the conflict are bound by the Second Protocol (of 1999) to the 1954 Hague Convention, Article 6(d) of the Protocol specifies that, in the event that cultural property becomes a military objective and there is no feasible alternative to attacking it, a party must give advance warning before an attack whenever circumstances permit.
2. Where cultural property is being used in support of military action, advance warning grants the opposing forces an opportunity to cease such use, with the consequence that the property will no longer constitute a military objective and must be spared attack. The warning should demand the termination of the use and give the opposing forces reasonable time to terminate such use.

3. Advance warning grants an opposing party an opportunity to take practical measures to minimize damage to the cultural property or to any movable cultural property housed in it, including by removing the latter to a place of safety or providing for adequate *in situ* protection (see Rule 134(a)).

Rule 133

(a) It is prohibited to launch an attack that may be expected to cause collateral damage to cultural property that would be excessive in relation to the concrete and direct military advantage anticipated.

Commentary

1. This Rule is based on the principle of proportionality, which is commented upon in general in paragraphs 1 and 6 of the Commentary to Rule 11 and in paragraph 1 of the Commentary to Rule 14. In the specific context of cultural property, the same substantive rule is codified in Article 7(c) of the Second Protocol to the 1954 Hague Convention. It is applicable in both international and non-international armed conflicts, in accordance with Articles 3 and 22(1) of the Second Protocol.
2. As applied to cultural property, the proportionality calculus involves qualitative as much as quantitative considerations. The measure of collateral damage to cultural property is a question not just of cubic metres but also of the cultural value of the property likely to be harmed. In this light, it is significant that movable or immovable property qualifying as cultural property is, by definition, of great importance to the cultural heritage of peoples (see Rule 130).

(b) Parties to the conflict must take feasible precautions in the choice of means and methods of attack with a view to avoiding, and in any event minimizing, collateral damage to cultural property.

Commentary

1. This Rule expresses the LOAC duty to take feasible precautions, which is commented upon in general in paragraphs 1 and 6 the Commentary to Rule 11 and in paragraph 1 of the Commentary to Rule 14. The corresponding duty is expressed in Article 7(b) of the Second Protocol (of 1999) to the 1954 Hague Convention for States Parties and is applicable in both international and non-international armed conflicts for such States, in accordance with Articles 3 and 22(1) of the Second Protocol.

Rule 134

Parties to the conflict liable to be attacked should, to the maximum extent feasible:

Commentary

1. Subparagraph (a) is derived from Article 8(a) of the Second Protocol (of 1999) to the 1954 Hague Convention, as well as Article 58(a) of AP/I and customary

LOAC. For parties to the conflict bound by the Second Protocol to the 1954 Hague Convention, the obligation in (a) is binding in both international and non-international armed conflict, by virtue of Articles 8(a) and 22(1) of the Second Protocol.

2. Subparagraph (b) is derived from Article 8(b) of the Second Protocol to the 1954 Hague Convention. For parties to the conflict bound by the Second Protocol to the 1954 Hague Convention, the obligation in (b) is binding in non-international armed conflict as well by virtue of Articles 8 (b) and 22(1) of the Second Protocol.

(a) Remove movable cultural property from the vicinity of military objectives or provide for adequate *in situ* protection; and

Commentary

1. The fact that the party subject to attack has not taken the precautions specified in Rule 134(a) does not relieve the attacking party of its obligations in attack under Rules 132 and 133.
2. The related rule in Article 3 of the 1954 Hague Convention stipulates that States Parties must take such measures as they consider appropriate to prepare in time of peace for the safeguarding of cultural property situated within their own territory against the foreseeable effects of armed conflict.

(b) Avoid locating military objectives near cultural property.

Commentary

1. Rule 134(b) requires, to the extent that the military situation and other relevant factors admit, that a party refrain from positioning in the vicinity of cultural property any likely military target. What is to be considered "near" cultural property depends on the circumstances of each case.
2. The fact that the party subject to attack has not taken the precautions specified in Rule 134(b) does not relieve the attacking party of its obligations in attack under Rules 132 and 133.

Rule 135

(a) Personnel exclusively engaged on behalf of a party to the conflict in the protection of cultural property should not be made the object of attack so far as is consistent with the security interests of the opposing party.

Commentary

1. Article 15 of the 1954 Hague Convention provides that, as far as is consistent with the security of the opposing party, personnel engaged in the protection of cultural property must, in the interest of such property, be respected. Cross-reference to Article 17(2)(b) and (c) of the Convention indicates that the

personnel in question are those engaged on behalf of a party to the conflict. One consequence of Article 15 is that such personnel must not be made the object of attack. This obligation is reflected in the present Rule.
2. The protection accorded by Rule 133(a) is available only if the relevant personnel are engaged exclusively in the protection of cultural property and not also, for example, in the protection of military objectives.
3. A party to the conflict may, in fulfilment of Article 3 of the 1954 Hague Convention and as expressly envisaged in Article 5 of the Second Protocol (of 1999), designate competent authorities responsible for the safeguarding of cultural property against the foreseeable effects of armed conflict. A party to the conflict may also, as implied by Article 8(4) of the Convention, specially empower "armed custodians" to guard cultural property. The Group of Experts were divided as to whether members of the armed forces may be engaged in the protection of cultural property and whether they would then be protected against attack.
4. It is unclear whether Article 15 of the 1954 Hague Convention extends to any members of a party's armed forces acting as "armed custodians" of cultural property within the meaning of Article 8(4) or to the "services or specialist personnel" established within a party's armed forces pursuant to Article 7(2).
5. In accordance with Article 21 of the Regulations for the Execution of the 1954 Hague Convention annexed to the Convention, personnel engaged in the protection of cultural property may wear an armlet bearing the distinctive emblem of cultural property (see Rule 136(a)), issued and stamped by the competent authorities of the State on whose behalf they are engaged, and must carry a special identity card bearing the emblem and the embossed stamp of the competent authorities. The precise appearance of the card is a matter for each State, although the information it contains is specified in Article 21 of the Regulations.

(b) Such personnel lose their protection if and for such time as they are directly participating in hostilities.

Commentary

1. The notion of DPH is addressed in general in chapter "Section VII: Civilians Directly Participating in Hostilities".

Rule 136

(a) Parties to the conflict may mark cultural property with a distinctive emblem.

Commentary

1. A distinctive emblem is created in Article 16(1) of the 1954 Hague Convention.

2. As provided for in Article 6 of the 1954 Hague Convention, States Parties to the Convention are expressly permitted to affix the emblem to or otherwise depict it on cultural property to facilitate the property's recognition as cultural property. This is reflected in Rule 136(a).
3. Article 17(4) of the Convention stipulates that the distinctive emblem may not be placed on any immovable cultural property unless at the same time there is displayed an authorization duly dated and signed by the competent authority of the State Party in question.
4. Distinctive marking of cultural property is not obligatory, either under Article 6 of the 1954 Hague Convention or under Rule 136(a). Consequently, the fact that property does not bear the emblem does not mean that it is not cultural property protected by the 1954 Hague Convention. Nor does it mean that it is not protected as cultural property under customary international law. In practice, the marking of cultural property with the distinctive emblem is rare.
5. It is not unlawful for a party to the conflict that is not a State Party to the 1954 Hague Convention to mark cultural property with the emblem.

(b) The deliberate misuse of the distinctive emblem in an armed conflict is prohibited.

Commentary

1. In accordance with both Article 17(3) of the 1954 Hague Convention and Article 38(1) of AP/I, and as restated in this Rule, the deliberate misuse during armed conflict of the distinctive emblem of cultural property is prohibited.

Rule 137

The foregoing rules are without prejudice to any 'special' or 'enhanced' protection in accordance with applicable treaties.

Commentary

1. This Rule preserves the prohibitions reflected in Article 8 of the 1954 Hague Convention ("special protection") and in Article 10 ff. of the Second Protocol (of 1999) to the 1954 Hague Convention ("enhanced protection").

Section XVI: Natural Environment

Rule 138
When planning and conducting military operations during an armed conflict, due regard should be given to the natural environment.

Commentary

1. According to Article 55(1), 1st sentence of AP/I, "care shall be taken in warfare to protect the natural environment against widespread, long-term and severe damage". However, several States have repeatedly declared that Article 55 does not reflect customary international law.[1]
2. Rule 44 of the Customary International Humanitarian Law Study (CIHL), applicable in international and arguably also in non-international armed conflicts, states that "methods and means of warfare must be employed with due regard to the protection and preservation of the natural environment".[2] The Group of Experts were of the view that the practice and *opinio juris* provided in support of Rule 44 CIHL were insufficient to establish a mandatory requirement of customary international law and that the word "should" was more appropriate.
3. Further objections have been made to the use of the phrase "due regard". It has been argued that the due regard standard is too broad to be of a customary nature in relation to care given to the natural environment during armed conflict.

---

[1]U.S Response to ICRC CIHL Study 521 ("France and the United States repeatedly have declared that Articles 35 (3) and 55 of AP/I, from which the Study derives the first sentence of rule 45, do not reflect customary international law. In their instrument of ratification of the 1980 CCW, both France and the United States asserted that the preambular paragraph in the CCW treaty, which refers to the substance of Articles 35 (3) and 55, applied only to states that have accepted those articles.

[2]CIHL, see chapter "Section XI: Destruction of Property", fn. 1, Rule 44 (1st sentence).

Y. Dinstein, A. W. Dahl, *Oslo Manual on Select Topics of the Law of Armed Conflict*,
https://doi.org/10.1007/978-3-030-39169-0_16

Rule 139
Rule 138 applies to the natural environment of:

(a) The Belligerent States,
(b) Neutral States,
(c) International sea areas, and
(d) Outer Space, the Moon and other Celestial Bodies (chapter "Section I: Outer Space").

Commentary

1. Since damage to the natural environment may easily transcend borders, the scope of Rule 138 is not limited to the territory of the Belligerent States and applies to all domains of warfare.
2. Outer Space, the Moon and other Celestial Bodies are defined in Rule 1.
3. It must be noted that it is controversial whether and to what extent Outer Space, the Moon and Other Celestial Bodies are considered to be parts of the natural environment for the purposes of LOAC.

Rule 140
In international armed conflict—subject to Rules 142 and 143—States should not use means and methods of warfare which are intended or may be expected to cause widespread, long-term and severe damage to the natural environment.

Commentary

1. Under AP/I, it is prohibited for States Parties to employ methods or means of warfare that are intended, or may be expected, to cause widespread, long-term and severe damage to the natural environment (Article 35(3)). In Article 55(1) of AP/I, a similar prohibition is stipulated. The latter provision identifies "the prohibition of the use of methods or means of warfare which are intended or may be expected to cause such damage to the natural environment and thereby to prejudice the health or survival of the population" as one of the manifestations of the duty of care in warfare to protect the natural environment.
2. Although protecting the environment during an international armed conflict—and taking into consideration the possible environmental implications of an attack—are incontrovertibly desirable as a matter of policy, some States have expressed the view that the AP/I prohibition does not constitute customary international law, with regard to either conventional or nuclear weapons.[3] That said, it is clear under the principle of distinction that parts of the natural environment cannot be made the object of attack unless they constitute military objectives. Further criticism of

[3]U.S Response to ICRC CIHL Study, see fn. 1.

AP/I is that it fails to acknowledge that, after a determination of military necessity and application of the distinction principle, the use of weapons causing damage to the natural environment is prohibited when it is expected to be excessive in relation to the concrete and direct overall military advantage anticipated.[4]

3. The interpretation of the terms "widespread", "long-term" and "severe" (which appear both in AP/I and in the ENMOD Convention[5]) is controversial. Moreover, it is agreed that the meaning of the words in one context (AP/I) is not the same as in other contexts (in particular the ENMOD Convention).
4. Although, in the view of the ICRC, the prohibition stipulated in Article 35(3) of AP/I is of customary nature, the assertion is not borne out by the available State practice and *opinio juris*. At the same time, there can hardly be any doubt that the issue of the protection of the environment in armed conflict has emerged as a particular international concern and that such a concern also manifests itself in the desirability of avoiding widespread, long-term and severe environmental damage. The practice and statements of several States, including those of States that are not Parties to AP/I, substantiate this concern.
5. Some States take the position that the application of this Rule is also subject to the principle of proportionality. These States rely, *inter alia,* on the terms of Article 8 (2)(b)(iv) of the Rome Statute of the International Criminal Court, 1998.

Rule 141
Under the ENMOD Convention, State Parties undertake not to engage in military or any other hostile use of environmental modification techniques having widespread, long-lasting or severe effects as the means of destruction, damage or injury to any other State Party.

Commentary

1. Under Articles 1 and 2 of the ENMOD Convention, States Parties undertake not to engage in "military or any other hostile use of environmental modification techniques [defined as any technique for changing—through the deliberate manipulation of natural processes—the dynamics, composition or structure of the Earth, including its biota, lithosphere, hydrosphere and atmosphere, or of Outer Space] having widespread, long-lasting or severe effects as the means of destruction, damage or injury to any other State Party". This means that States will refrain from using the environment itself as a weapon when fighting another State Party to the ENMOD Convention.

---

[4] *Ibid*

[5] See chapter "Section I: Outer Space", fn. 19.

2. Rule 45 of the CIHL, which stipulates a prohibition of the use of the "destruction of the natural environment [. . .] as a weapon", is based, *inter alia*, on the ENMOD Convention. However, the CIHL itself describes the customary status of the ENMOD Convention as "unclear".[6]

Rule 142
Intentional destruction of any part of the natural environment qualifying as a civilian object is prohibited, unless required by imperative military necessity.

Commentary

1. Destruction of property when required by imperative military necessity is dealt with in general in chapter "Section XI: Destruction of Property" with accompanying Commentary.
2. The present Rule reflects the widely accepted view that the prohibition against the destruction or seizure of enemy property, unless required by military necessity, can be extended to apply to those parts of the natural environment that constitute civilian objects.
3. It must be borne in mind that the prohibition of the intentional destruction of the natural environment is contingent on consideration of military necessity. Absent military necessity, such destruction cannot be justified.
4. On the other hand, it has been argued that no sufficient State practice or *opinio juris* in support of this position (which extends the customary prohibition against destruction of enemy property as set out in chapter "Section XI: Destruction of Property") exists.
5. Although the wording of the present Rule 142 is broad, it is agreed that *de minimis* damage, such as the destruction of a single tree, does not constitute a violation of this Rule. It is unclear at what point destruction is no longer considered *de minimis* and comes within the application of the Rule as stated.

Rule 143
Although parts of the natural environment constitute civilian objects other parts may be regarded as military objectives by location, purpose or use (e.g., camouflage).

Commentary

1. Many portions of the natural environment may be viewed presumptively as civilian objects. Still, there are two schools of thought in this matter. One school of thought regards the natural environment as worthy of protection *per se*. Another school of thought, anthropocentric in nature, focuses on those portions

---

[6]CIHL, see chapter "Section XI: Destruction of Property", fn. 1, vol. I, page 155.

of the natural environment that human beings are dependent on for their survival or health.

2. However extensively the inherently protected portions of the natural environment are viewed, it cannot be denied that—due to purpose, location or use—parts of the environment can qualify as military objectives. This is expressly recognized in Protocol III of the CCW Convention, which lays down in Article 2(4): "It is prohibited to make forests or other kinds of plant cover the object of attack by incendiary weapons except when such natural elements are used to cover, conceal or camouflage combatants or other military objectives, or are themselves military objectives".

Rule 144
Feasible precautions should be taken to avoid, or in any event to minimize, incidental damage to parts of the natural environment constituting civilian objects.

Commentary

1. The general principle for States Parties to AP/I, as stated in Article 57(1), is that parties to an armed conflict must take constant care to spare civilian objects. This principle extends to the natural environment, if and when it constitutes a civilian object.
2. Constant care includes the notion of taking feasible precautions in attack to avoid or minimize incidental damage to those parts of the environment that constitute civilian objects.

Rule 145
It is prohibited to launch an attack against a lawful target, which may be expected to cause incidental damage to those parts of the natural environment that constitute civilian objects, expected to be excessive in relation to the concrete and direct overall military advantage anticipated.

Commentary

1. This Rule expresses the principle of proportionality, which is commented upon in general terms in paragraph 1 of the Commentary to Rule 11. Several States, including some not party to AP/I, have accepted the obligation to include expected environmental damage in the proportionality assessment of a proposed attack. In a similar vein, the ICJ had earlier observed that "States must take environmental considerations into account when assessing what is necessary and proportionate in the pursuit of legitimate military objectives. Respect for the

environment is one of the elements that go to assessing whether an action is in conformity with the principles of necessity and proportionality."[7]

2. However, the Rule applies only to parts of the natural environment constituting civilian objects. For example, where the natural environment is used for camouflage or as a shield for armed forces (see Rule 143), that part of the natural environment may be considered a military objective by use or location. With regard to destruction of parts of the natural environment as a consequence of movement of military forces, see chapter "Section XI: Destruction of Property" with Commentary.

[7] ICJ Advisory Opinions in the *Nuclear Weapons Case,* see chapter "Outer Space", fn. 8, para 30.

Section XVII: International Criminal Law

Rule 146
Those who decide upon, plan, order or execute military operations during an armed conflict bear individual criminal responsibility for war crimes they have committed.

Commentary

1. Under International Criminal Law (ICL), persons may be individually accountable for international crimes (e.g., war crimes, crimes against humanity and genocide) provided, *inter alia*, that the following basic conditions are satisfied:

   a. That the conduct, at the time it took place, constituted a crime according to law, referred to as the principle of *nullum crimen sine lege.*[1]
   b. That punishment can only be imposed following a conviction in accordance with the principle of *nulla poena sine lege.*[2]
   c. That they are not to be tried twice for the same conduct that formed the basis for the crime, referred to as the principle of *ne bis in idem.*[3]
   d. That they acted with the mental element(s) required for the specific crime and that no situation existed to negate the element(s).[4]
   e. That there are no reasons to exclude criminal responsibility (e.g., self-defence or mental disease).[5]

[1]Expressed in the Rome Statute, see chapter "Section XI: Destruction of Property", fn. 1, Article 22.
[2]Expressed in the Rome Statute, *ibid,* Article 23.
[3]Expressed in the Rome Statute, *ibid,* Article 20.
[4]Expressed in the Rome Statute, *ibid,* Articles 30 and 32.
[5]Expressed in the Rome Statute, *ibid,* Article 31.

Y. Dinstein, A. W. Dahl, *Oslo Manual on Select Topics of the Law of Armed Conflict*,
https://doi.org/10.1007/978-3-030-39169-0_17

2. This chapter deals only with war crimes. However, it must be borne in mind that a war crime may also constitute a crime against humanity or genocide.
3. The construct of "war crimes" is well embedded in customary international law as confirmed by the judgment of the International Military Tribunal at Nuremburg. War crimes have been defined by the 1998 Rome Statute of the International Criminal Court for the purposes of that treaty. However, Article 10 of the Rome Statute provides that the definition of war crimes in that treaty shall not be interpreted as limiting or prejudicing in any way existing or developing rules of international law. Some States apply different definitions of war crimes under customary international law.
4. The reference to "decide upon, plan, order or execute" is understood to encompass, in principle, the whole spectrum of involvement in military operations. This includes individuals who assist in the commission of conduct constituting a crime and who may, depending on the circumstances, be guilty of aiding and abetting a crime.[6] The mere presence in a place where an international crime occurs does not in itself amount to a commission of that crime. See, in this regard, Rule 147 on the notion of command responsibility.
5. The text of the Rome Statute binds only States Parties. Irrespective of the Statute, war crimes are incorporated in the domestic criminal law of many States. In many instances, States punish war criminals through the ordinary application of their criminal law by using common domestic offences such as murder or assault. Although a war crime can only be committed within the context of an armed conflict (whether international or non-international), a crime against humanity or genocide can be committed outside situations of armed conflict.

Rule 147
Military commanders bear individual criminal responsibility if they knew or, owing to the circumstances at the time, had reason to know that their subordinates were committing, were about to commit, or had committed any war crime, and failed to take necessary and reasonable measures to prevent their commission or to punish the perpetrators thereof.

Commentary

1. This Rule addresses command responsibility, *i.e.* the responsibility of superiors for acts committed by their subordinates. However, all commanders obviously also bear direct responsibility for their own actions under Rule 146.
2. This Rule is derived from case law after WWII (in particular, the "Subsequent Proceedings" at Nuremburg and the judgment of the International Military Tribunal for the Far East at Tokyo). The construct of command responsibility has been codified in Article 7(3) of the Statute of the ICTY, Article 6(3) of the

[6]See Rome Statute, *ibid,* Article 25.

Statute of the ICTR, as well as Article 28 of the Rome Statute. Although this construct is embedded in customary international law, the Rome Statute articulation of command responsibility is binding only in the application of the Rome Statute itself.

3. Command responsibility is applicable in both international and non-international armed conflict.
4. Command responsibility relies on three cumulative criteria: (a) the superior-subordinate relationship between the commander and the forces under his or her effective control; (b) the fact that the commander or superior knew or had reason to know about the crimes or potential crimes in the circumstances at the time; and (c) the commander or superior's failure to take necessary and reasonable measures to prevent or punish the crimes.
5. Article 28(b) of the Rome Statute applies a similar rule to civilian superiors provided that a clear link is established between the crimes committed by subordinates and the effective authority and control of the civilian superiors. Similarly, with respect to the attribution of knowledge to the civilian superior, there is a strict requirement of conscious disregard of the information available.
6. Commanders may be punished directly for their failure to take necessary and reasonable measures to ensure that their subordinates do not commit violations of LOAC.
7. Command responsibility is not a form of strict liability. The commander's personal dereliction of duty must have contributed to or failed to prevent the offence committed by his subordinates. There must be a personal neglect amounting to a wanton, disregard of the action of his or her subordinates amounting to a crime *per se.*

Rule 148
The fact that a war crime has been committed by a person pursuant to an order of a Government or of a superior, whether military or civilian, does not, as such, relieve that person of criminal responsibility.

Commentary

1. This Rule is based on Nuremberg Principle IV,[7] which reflects customary ICL, as distinct from the rule in Article 33 of the Rome Statute which provides for an exclusion of criminal responsibility if specified circumstances apply.
2. The fact that a war crime has been committed under superior orders may be considered in mitigation of punishment. Mitigation of punishment may also depend on a variety of other circumstances the accused was acting under, e.g., the gravity of the crime, his/her rank, and knowledge of the overall military operation that the

---

[7]Principles of International Law Recognized in the Charter of the Nuremberg Tribunal and in the Judgment of the Tribunal, Adopted by the International Law Commission of the United Nations (Nuremberg Principles) (1950), *The Laws of Armed Conflicts*, page 1265.

conduct was a part of, as well as military experience and what could reasonably have been expected from a soldier in a similar situation.
3. The phrase "as such" was added in order to emphasize that other circumstances may preclude criminal responsibility, as referred to in paragraph 1 of the Commentary to Rule 146.

Rule 149
A person's official position does not relieve that person of criminal responsibility for a war crime.

Commentary

1. This Rule is based on Nuremberg Principle III, later repeated in Article 27 of the Rome Statute, as well as Article 7(2) of the Statute of the ICTY and Article 6 (2) of the Statute of the ICTR. "Official position" includes that of both Heads of State as well as other governmental officials.

Rule 150
No statutory limitation applies to certain war crimes, irrespective of the date of their commission.

Commentary

1. The 1968 Convention on the Non-Applicability of Statutory Limitations to War Crimes and Crimes against Humanity, as well as the European Convention on the Non-Applicability of Statutory Limitations to Crimes against Humanity and War Crimes, prohibit statutory limitations with regard to certain international crimes.[8] The same prohibition is repeated in Article 29 of the Rome Statute.
2. The non-application of statutory limitation applies to traditional war crimes, as defined in Article 1(a) of the 1968 Convention. There is no sufficient State practice indicating that it can be extended to other war crimes.

Rule 151
Any person charged with a war crime has the right to be tried by an impartial and regularly constituted court respecting the generally recognized principles of regular judicial procedure.

Commentary

1. This wording expresses customary law minimum fair trial guarantees and is based on the wording of Article 75 of AP/I. Minimum fair trial guarantees must be

---

[8]Convention on the Non-Applicability of Statutory Limitations to War Crimes and Crimes Against Humanity (1968), *Laws of Armed Conflict*, page 1267, Article 1. European Convention on the Non-Applicability of Statutory Limitations to Crimes Against Humanity and War Crimes (1974), *Laws of Armed Conflicts*, page 1281, Article 1.

enforced in any prosecution of any crime, including war crimes, crimes against humanity or genocide.
2. The phrase "regularly constituted court" appears in Common Article 3 of the Geneva Conventions and is repeated in the Rome Statute of the International Criminal Court.
3. The generally recognized principles of regular judicial procedure include, *inter alia:*[9]

   a. The right to be informed without delay, in an understandable language, of the particulars of the offence alleged against him/her.
   b. The right not to be convicted by a tribunal or a court that does not satisfy the basic conditions mentioned in paragraph 1 of the Commentary to Rule 146.
   c. The right to be presumed innocent until proved guilty according to law.
   d. The right to be tried in his/her own presence with the necessary rights and means of defence.
   e. The right not to be compelled to testify against himself/herself or to confess guilt.

Rule 152
Individual criminal responsibility for war crimes may lead to penal proceedings before competent international, domestic or hybrid courts.

Commentary
1. Many States are currently bound by the 1998 Rome Statute of the International Criminal Court. However, many States are not Contracting Parties to the Rome Statute, and have not accepted its jurisdiction in respect of their personnel. For example, the United States has rejected any assertion of ICC jurisdiction over nationals that are not parties to the Rome Statute, absent a UN Security Council referral or the consent of that State.[10]
2. Hybrid courts are characterized by both international and domestic elements and have been established, *inter alia,* in Sierra Leone and Cambodia.
3. Proceedings before an international court or tribunal or a hybrid court are subject to the respective statute establishing the forum.
4. War crimes proceedings before international and domestic courts are subject to jurisdictional limitations and immunities imposed by international law.
5. A crucial issue in trials before international and domestic courts is whether there exists universal jurisdiction over war crimes. The issue is controversial, and the Group of Experts decided not to address it.
6. Domestic and international courts must observe applicable jurisdictional immunities found in international law. In this regard, it should be pointed out that the

[9]See for example AP/I, chapter "Section I: Outer Space", fn. 13, Article 75(3) and (4).
[10]U.S Statement to the 16th Sessions of the Assembly of States Parties to the Rome Statute.

International Court of Justice, in the *Arrest Warrant* case, recognized immunities from foreign jurisdictions for high-ranking officials (in that case, a Foreign Minister).[11] Jurisdictional immunity under international law is subject to waiver by the respective State.

7. The enforcement of international criminal law by international or foreign courts is subject to the fundamental principles of complementarity and subsidiarity, respectively. Accordingly, the State with the strongest jurisdictional links to a particular incident should be given the opportunity to conduct criminal proceedings. Only if it does not do so, or is unwilling or unable to do so, international or foreign proceeding would be considered a legitimate course of action.

[11] Arrest Warrant of 11 April 2000 (Democratic Republic of the Congo v. Belgium), Judgment, *I.C. J. Reports* 2002, page 3, para 51–52 and 61.

Section XVIII: Extraterritorial Operations Against Non-state Armed Groups

Rule 153
The right of self-defence applies in response to an armed attack by non-State armed groups.

Commentary

1. The exercise of the right of self-defence in response to an armed attack by non-State armed groups is demonstrated by the general practice and *opinio juris* of States in reaction to the events of September 11, 2001. This has been confirmed, *inter alia,* by Security Council resolutions (1368 and 1373) and by international organizations such as NATO.

Rule 154
A State may exercise its right of self-defence against non-State armed groups in a foreign State in response to an armed attack mounted by them from outside the victim State's territory, subject to the Charter of the United Nations.

Commentary

1. This Rule does not address the issue of domestic terrorism.
2. It might not be possible or necessary to distinguish between armed attacks launched by another State as such (whether it is carried out by *de jure* or *de facto* organs), on the one hand, and armed attacks carried out by non-State armed groups, on the other. The inherent right of self-defence, enshrined in Article 51 of the Charter of the United Nations, is not contingent on armed attack being attributable to another State.
3. If the foreign State knowingly provides shelter to the armed group, or otherwise connives with it, an armed attack carried out by the armed group it may bear responsibility for such actions.

Y. Dinstein, A. W. Dahl, *Oslo Manual on Select Topics of the Law of Armed Conflict*,
https://doi.org/10.1007/978-3-030-39169-0_18

4. An armed attack by non-State armed groups may be launched from foreign territory, where there is no connivance by the territorial State notwithstanding the fact that the armed group has its base of operations within that territory. If the victim State exercises its right of self-defence, it will likely do so within the territory of the State in which such base of operation is situated. Nevertheless, the exercise of self-defence will be directed against the non-state armed groups and not against the foreign State itself.

Rule 155
Self-defence may be exercised in the circumstances referred to in Rule 154 without the consent of the incumbent territorial Government if the latter is unable or unwilling to take the action necessary to suppress armed attacks by a non-State armed group against the victim State.

Commentary

1. This mode of non-consensual self-defence is in conformity with the general practice of States and the Charter of the United Nations. It is sometimes called "extra-territorial law enforcement", which is permissible when a local Government is unable or unwilling to suppress armed attacks carried out by non-State armed groups against foreign States.
2. Admittedly, the scale of the use of force in self-defence against the "Islamic State" within Syria—by the U.S-led coalition, operating without the consent or invitation of the Syrian Government—is extraordinary.
3. As in all other instances of self-defence, the exercise of the right has to be carried out in accordance with the customary conditions of necessity, proportionality and immediacy.

Rule 156
The right of self-defence against non-State armed groups in the circumstances referred to in Rule 154 may be exercised either individually or collectively.

Commentary

1. The United States and other members of the international coalition have justified their military operations in Syria against the "Islamic State" on the ground of collective self-defence in response to an armed attack against Iraq.
2. In the meantime, the "Islamic State" has carried out numerous armed attacks against other countries. Most of the members of the large coalition that has been operating against the "Islamic State" have been acting in collective self-defence.
3. Some other members of the coalition fighting the "Islamic State" may have different rationales for their operations in Syria.

Rule 157
The extra-territorial exercise of the right of self-defence against non-State armed groups does not *per se* bring into existence an international armed conflict.

Commentary

1. Broadly speaking, the armed conflict in Syria (beginning in 2011) constitutes a clear illustration of the application of this Rule.
2. The rationale is that the States conducting operations in Syria are engaged in fighting there either by invitation of the Syrian Government or—if operating without such invitation—they are confronting non-State armed groups in an exercise of the right of individual or collective self-defence against an armed attack.
3. The crux of the matter is that (broadly speaking) there have been no hostilities *between* States in Syria (in other words, the States belonging to the anti-"Islamic State" coalition and the Syrian Government have largely chosen not to engage one another with military force).
4. Despite the allegations of some, it should be stressed that the Syrian hostilities have not generated a new LOAC matrix by adding a third category to the existing dichotomy of international armed conflicts and non-international armed conflicts.

Appendix A: Group of Experts

1. **Air Commodore (ret.) William H. Boothby**
   Associate Fellow,
   Geneva Centre for Security Policy
2. **Michel Bourbonniere, QC**
   Counsel
   Canadian Space Agency, legal services
3. **Professor Laurie Blank**
   Director
   Emory University School of Law
4. **Judge Advocate General Lars Morten Bjørkholt**
   Judge Advocate General
   Office of the Judge Advocate General for the Norwegian Armed Forces, Oslo
5. **Professor Geoffrey Corn**
   Presidential Research Professor of Law
   South Texas College of Law Houston
6. **Judge Advocate General (ret.) Arne Willy Dahl**
   Project Manager
   Judge Advocate General (ret.)
   Office of the Judge Advocate General for the Norwegian Armed Forces, Oslo
7. **Prof. Dr. Yoram Dinstein (ret.)**
   Academic Director,
   Professor Emeritus of International Law
   Tel Aviv University
8. **Professor Magne Frostad**
   Arctic University of Tromsoe
9. **Prof. Dr. Wolff Heintschel von Heinegg**
   Dean of the Faculty of Law and Professor of International Law
   Europa-University Viadrina, Frankfurt (Oder)

Y. Dinstein, A. W. Dahl, *Oslo Manual on Select Topics of the Law of Armed Conflict*,
https://doi.org/10.1007/978-3-030-39169-0

10. **Sigrid Redse Johansen (PhD)**
    Associate professor
    Norwegian Defence University College
11. **Professor Jann Kleffner**
    Professor of International Law and Head of the International Law Centre
    Swedish Defence University.
12. **Attorney William Lietzau**
13. **Professor Roger O'Keefe**
    Professor of Public International Law
    University College London
14. **Professor Marco Roscini**
    Professor of International Law
    University of Westminster
15. **Brigadier General (ret), Jan Peter Spijk**
    Military Legal Services, Royal Netherlands Army (ret.)
    President, International Society for Military Law and the Law of War

Appendix B: Members of the Drafting Committee

- Arne Willy Dahl
- Yoram Dinstein (Chair)
- Wolff Heintschel von Heinegg
- William Lietzau
- Sigrid Redse Johansen[1]
- William Boothby[2]

[1]Until March 2018

[2]From December 2017

Y. Dinstein, A. W. Dahl, *Oslo Manual on Select Topics of the Law of Armed Conflict*,
https://doi.org/10.1007/978-3-030-39169-0

The manufacturer's authorised representative in the EU is Springer Nature Customer Service Centre GmbH, Europaplatz 3, 69115 Heidelberg, Germany. If you have any concerns regarding our products, please contact ProductSafety@springernature.com

Printed and bound by CPI Group (UK) Ltd, Croydon, CR0 4YY
05/10/2026
02228154-0006